全日本空手道剛柔会

剛柔流型教本
下巻

Japan Karatedo Gojukai Association
Goju-ryu Kata series (vol.2)

目次　Contents

転掌

テンショウ

Tensho

型のポイント

　「三戦」と共に剛柔流を代表する型で、「三戦」の剛に対して「転掌」は柔に例えて表現される。
　呼吸法"息吹"は原則的には「三戦」と同じで、剛と柔すなわち陽と陰の息吹で修練することが出来る。ただし「三戦」よりも円運動が主になるので、息吹は柔らかめになり、肘と手首によるスムーズな軌道と丹田からの意識の流れが伴わなければならない。
　息吹の順序は「三戦」と同じ"呑（吸）"・"吐（呼）"による陽息吹で行うが、年配者には陰息吹、半陽陰息吹で行うことを勧めている。
　呼吸とは吐いてから吸うべき順番であることから、"呑"から始める呼吸の前後には"耐"が入ることが望ましい。また"吐"の後に"極"で横隔膜を締めることによって腹式呼吸が容易になる。
　第3挙動から第5挙動、第13挙動から第15挙動、第23挙動から第25挙動の外掛け受け、内掛け受けは一回の"呑"で外内掛け受けを通しで行う呼吸法もあるが、本書では、"呑"を二度続け呼吸する。慣れたら通しの息吹でも出来るようになる。
　第32挙動から第34挙動の両手掬い受けから両手張り突きは短く吸って、短く吐く呼吸法もある。本書は「三戦」の息吹に合わせて、ゆっくり吸って、ゆっくり吐く息吹にて行っている。
　全ての"息吹"はゆっくりまたは速く、長くそして短く、それぞれ調整が可能である。

This is the another typical kata of Goju-ryu, similar to Sanchin. It is described as " 柔 "
(Ju, to be soft) in contrast with Sanchin which is described as " 剛 " (Go, to be hard).
Tensho's breathing method Ibuki is same as Sanchin's in principle, and it can be trained with
both 剛 (Go) Ibuki and 柔 (Ju) Ibuki, namely, 陽 (Yo, the positive) and 陰 (In, the negative).
However, Ibuki in Tensho must be softer because of circular movements.
Also proper circular movements as well as focus on moving energy from Tanden to various parts
of the body is required to perform Tensho correctly.
Yo Ibuki (strong breathing) , which is done by "Don (inhale)" and "To(exhale)", is used in Tensho
as well as Sanchin. However, In Ibuki (soft breathing) and Han Yo In Ibuki (medium strength
breathing) are recommended for elders.
Since one must exhale before breathing in, it is desirable that "Tai (pause)" comes before the
breathing starting from "Don (inhale)". Also, tensing one's diaphragm as "Kyoku (kime or focus)"
after "To (exhale)" makes abdominal respiration easier.
Some perform Soto Kakeuke and Uchi Kakeuke in the following pages (motion number 3-5,
13-15, and 23-25) with one continuous "Don". In this manual, the method used is to use a
separate "Don" for each technique. As one's skill increases, one can perform the first method,
with one continuous "Don" for both techniques.
The part with double arm Sukui Uke into double arm Hari Tsuki (motion number 32-34) can
be performed with short "Don" and short "To". This manual shows another method using long
"Don" and long "To" as well as Sanchin's Ibuki method.
All Ibuki can be adjusted to be either slow or quick, as well as long or short.
※
Don : to inhale
To : to exhale
Tai : to pause
Kyoku : Kime or focus

気を付け	礼	気を付け

立ち方●結び立ち
注意点●顎を引き、両手は真っすぐ
伸ばして大腿側部につける
Stance ● Musubidachi
Point ● Pull chin back. Keep
fingers straight and hands on
outer thight

立ち方●結び立ち
注意点●前方30度位、礼は深すぎ
ない
Stance ● Musubidachi
Point ● Bow forward for 30° .Be
careful not to bow too deeply

立ち方●結び立ち
Stance ● Musubidachi

【掛け合わせ】
Kake Awase

用意1　　　　　　用意2　　　　　　用意3

中間動作

裏側

立ち方●結び立ち
注意点●右掌内側、丹田の前で重ね
集中
息吹●ゆっくり呑
Stance ● Musubidachi
Point ● Right hand on the inside.
Hands are crossed in front of
Tanden
Ibuki ● Inhale slowly

立ち方●平行立ち
注意点●爪先を支点に踵を外に開く
Stance ● Heiko Dachi
Point ● Keep balls of feet in
place and only move heels

立ち方●平行立ち
注意点●両拳は脇を締めながら体側
へ、正拳は真下へ向けて、両肩を落
とす
息吹●ゆっくり吐
Stance ● Heiko Dachi
Point ● Keep elbows against
side of body, fists pointing
straight down, and shoulders
relaxed
Ibuki ● Exhale slowly

北 N

W 西 ——— 東 E

南 S

第１挙動	第２挙動	第３挙動

立ち方●右三戦立ち
技●三戦の構え　右腕外側より両手中段受け
注意点●右足を内側中心線より一歩前進
息吹●呑・吐
Stance ● Right Sanchin Dachi
Tech. ● Do double arm Chudan Uke into Sanchin No Kamae. Right arm is on the outside when blocking
Point ● Step forward w/ right foot using an inward curve
Ibuki ● Don and To

立ち方●右三戦立ち
技●左拳引き手
Stance ● Right Sanchin Dachi
Tech. ● Left Hikite

立ち方●右三戦立ち
技●右拳を返して右掌外掛け受け
注意点●受けは右中心線
息吹●呑
Stance ● Right Sanchin Dachi
Tech. ● Turn right fist over into right Soto Kakeuke
Point ● Block is in center of right half of body
Ibuki ● Don

第４挙動　　　　第５挙動

立ち方●右三戦立ち
技●右掌内掛け受け　引き手
注意点●右中心線を受けて引き手は
掌が正面。指先は上向き
息吹●呑
Stance ● Right Sanchin Dachi
Tech. ● Right Uchi Kakeuke (
open hand) into Hikite
Point ● Block is in center of
right half of body. Hikite palm is
facing front and fingers are facing up
Ibuki ● Don

立ち方●右三戦立ち
技●右掌底掌当て
注意点●右中心線、鎖骨の高さに当て
息吹●吐
Stance ● Right Sanchin Dachi
Tech. ● Right Teisho Ate
Point ● Ate is in center of right
half of body at collarbone height
Ibuki ● To

第6挙動   第7挙動   第8挙動

立ち方●右三戦立ち
技●右掌外掛け落とし　引き手
注意点●右中心線を受け　引き手は
掌が正面。指先は下向き
息吹●呑

Stance ● Right Sanchin Dachi
Tech. ● Right Soto Kake Otoshi
(open hand) into Hikite
Point ● Block is in center of
right half of body. Hikite palm is
facing front and fingers are facing down
Ibuki ● Don

立ち方●右三戦立ち
技●右掌下段底掌当て
注意点●右中心線　鼠蹊部(そけいぶ)
息吹●吐

Stance ● Right Sanchin Dachi
Tech. ● Right Gedan Teisho Ate
Point ● Ate is in center of right
half of body. Hit to the groin
Ibuki ● To

立ち方●右三戦立ち
技●右掌を返して　鶴頭上げ受け
注意点●右中心線　高さ三戦の構え。
親指は内、中指薬指に合わせる
息吹●呑

Stance ● Right Sanchin Dachi
Tech. ● Turn right hand over
into Kakuto Age Uke
Point ● Block is in center of
right half of body. Hand is the
same height as Sanchin No
Kamae. Keep thumb pressed
together the middle finger and
ring finger
Ibuki ● Don

第9挙動

第10挙動

中間動作

裏側

立ち方●右三戦立ち
技●右掌を返して　底掌落とし受け
注意点●右中心線肘の高さまで　掌は縦、指先は上に真っすぐ
息吹●吐
Stance ● Right Sanchin Dachi
Tech. ● Turn right hand over into Teisho Otoshi Uke
Point ● Block is in center of right half of body, hand is at elbow height. Fingers are facing straight up
Ibuki ● To

立ち方●右三戦立ち
技●右掌を返して　鶴頭外受け
注意点●右中心線の受け　肘の高さ。掌を手首でなびかせ、肘は三戦構え
息吹●呑
Stance ● Right Sanchin Dachi
Tech. ● Turn right hand over from the wrist into Kakuto Soto Uke
Point ● Block is in center of right half of body at elbow height. Elbow position is same as Sanchin No Kamae
Ibuki ● Don

第 11 挙動	第 12 挙動	第 13 挙動

立ち方●右三戦立ち
技●右掌を返して　底掌内受け
注意点●右中心線の位置まて。掌は
肘の高さ。掌を手首でなびかせ、肘
は三戦構え
息吹●吐
Stance ● Right Sanchin Dachi
Tech. ● Turn right hand over from
the wrist into Teisho Uchi Uke
Point ● Block stops in the center of right half of body at elbow
height. Elbow position is same
as Sanchin No Kamae
Ibuki ● To

立ち方●左三戦立ち
技●左腕中段受け
注意点●左足を一歩前進　左拳は右
肘下から
息吹●なし
Stance ● Left Sanchin Dachi
Tech. ● Chudan Uke w/ left arm
Point ● Step forward w/ left
foot. Left hand goes under right
elbow when blocking
Ibuki ● No Ibuki

立ち方●左三戦立ち
技●左拳を返して　左掌外掛け受け
注意点●受けは左中心線
息吹●呑
Stance ● Left Sanchin Dachi
Tech. ● Turn left fist over into
left Soto Kakeuke
Point ● Block is in center of left
half of body
Ibuki ● Don

第14挙動　　　　　第15挙動

裏側

立ち方●左三戦立ち
技●左掌内掛け受け　引き手
注意点●左中心線を受けて引き手は
掌が正面。指先は上向き
息吹●呑
Stance ● Left Sanchin Dachi
Tech. ● Left Uchi Kakeuke into
Hikite
Point ● Block is in center of left
half of body. Palm facing front.
Fingers facing up
Ibuki ● Don

立ち方●左三戦立ち
技●左掌底掌当て
注意点●左中心線、鎖骨の高さに当て
息吹●吐
Stance ● Left Sanchin Dachi
Tech. ● Left Teisho Ate (open
hand)
Point ● Ate is in center of left
half of body at collarbone height
Ibuki ● To

第16挙動　　　第17挙動　　　第18挙動

立ち方●左三戦立ち
技●左掌外掛け落とし　引き手
注意点●左中心線を受け。引き手は
掌が正面、指先は下向き
息吹●呑

Stance ● Left Sanchin Dachi
Tech. ● Left Soto Kake Otoshi
(open hand) into Hikite
Point ● Block (Otoshi) is in
center of left half of body. Hikte
palm is facing front and fingers
are facing down
Ibuki ● Don

立ち方●左三戦立ち
技●左掌下段底掌当て
注意点●左中心線　鼠蹊部(そけいぶ)
息吹●吐

Stance ● Left Sanchin Dachi
Tech. ● Left Gedan Teisho Ate
Point ● Ate is in center of left
half of body. Hit to the groin
Ibuki ● To

立ち方●左三戦立ち
技●左掌を返して　鶴頭上げ受け
注意点●左中心線。高さは三戦の構
え。親指は内、中指薬指に合わせる
息吹●呑

Stance ● Left Sanchin Dachi
Tech. ● Turn left hand over into
Kakuto Age Uke
Point ● Block is in center of left
half of body and hand is the same
height as Sanchin No Kamae.
Keep thumb pressed together
middle finger and ring finger
Ibuki ● Don

第 19 挙動	第 20 挙動	第 21 挙動

中間動作

裏側

立ち方●左三戦立ち	立ち方●左三戦立ち	立ち方●左三戦立ち
技●左掌を返して 底掌落とし受け	技●左掌を返して 鶴頭外受け	技●左掌を返して 底掌内受け
注意点●左中心線肘の高さまで。掌は縦、指先は上に真っすぐ	注意点●左中心線を受け。肘の高さ。掌を手首でなびかせ、肘は三戦構え	注意点●左中心線の位置まで。掌は肘の高さ。掌を手首でなびかせ、肘は三戦の構え
息吹●吐	息吹●呑	息吹●吐
Stance ● Left Sanchin Dachi	Stance ● Left Sanchin Dachi	Stance ● Left Sanchin Dachi
Tech. ● Turn left hand over into Teisho Otoshi Uke	Tech. ● Turn left hand over from the wrist into Kakuto Soto Uke	Tech. ● Turn left hand over from the wrist into Teisho Uchi Uke
Point ● Block is in center of left half of body, hand is at elbow height. Fingers are facing straight up	Point ● Block is in center of left half of body, at elbow height. Left elbow position is same as Sanchin No Kamae	Point ● Block stops at center of left half of body at elbow height. Elbow position is same as Sanchin No Kamae
Ibuki ● To	Ibuki ● Don	Ibuki ● To

第22挙動　　　第23挙動

立ち方●右三戦立ち
技●両腕中段受け　三戦の構え
注意点●右足を一歩前進。右拳は左腕の外側から交差構え
息吹●なし

Stance ● Right Sanchin Dachi
Tech. ● Double arm Chudan Uke into Sanchin No Kamae
Point ● Step forward w/ right foot. Right hand is on the outside when blocking
Ibuki ● No Ibuki

立ち方●右三戦立ち
技●両拳を返して　両掌掛け受け
注意点●受けは左右中心線。両肘は三戦構え
息吹●呑

Stance ● Right Sanchin Dachi
Tech. ● Turn fists over into double arm Kakeuke
Point ● Blocks are in center of left/right half of body. Elbow position is same as Sanchin No Kamae
Ibuki ● Don

第24挙動　　　第25挙動

中間動作

裏側

立ち方●右三戦立ち
技●両掌内掛け受け　引き手
注意点●左右中心線を受けて引き手は掌が正面。指先は上向き
息吹●呑
Stance ● Right Sanchin Dachi
Tech. ● Uchi Kakeuke w/ both hands into Hikite
Point ● Block center of right/left half of body. Hikite palm is facing front and fingers are facing up
Ibuki ● Don

立ち方●右三戦立ち
技●両掌底掌当て
注意点●左右中心線、鎖骨の高さに当て
息吹●吐
Stance ● Right Sanchin Dachi
Tech. ● Double arm Teisho Ate
Point ● Hit center of left/right half of body at collarbone height
Ibuki ● To

第26挙動 　　　　　第27挙動 　　　　　第28挙動

立ち方●右三戦立ち
技●両掌外掛け落とし　引き手
注意点●左右中心線を受け。引き手
は掌が正面、指先は下向き
息吹●呑
Stance ● Right Sanchin Dachi
Tech. ● Soto Kake Otoshi w/
both hands into Hikite
Point ● Blocks are in center
of left/right half of body. Hikite
palm is facing front and fingers
are facing down
Ibuki ● Don

立ち方●右三戦立ち
技●両掌下段底掌当て
注意点●左右中心線　鼠蹊部（そけ
いぶ）
息吹●吐
Stance ● Right Sanchin Dachi
Tech. ● Double arm Gedan
Teisho Ate
Point ● Double Ate are center
of left/right half of body. Hit to
the groin
Ibuki ● To

立ち方●右三戦立ち
技●両手を返して　鶴頭上げ受け
注意点●左右中心線　高さは三戦の
構え。親指は内、中指薬指に合わせる
息吹●呑
Stance ● Right Sanchin Dachi
Tech. ● Turn hands over into
Kakuto Age Uke
Point ● Blocks are center of left/
right half of body and are the same
height as Sanchin No Kamae.
Keep thumb, pressed together
middle finger and ring finger
Ibuki ● Don

第29挙動	第30挙動	第31挙動

中間動作

裏側

立ち方●右三戦立ち
技●両掌を返して　底掌落とし受け
注意点●左右中心線　肘の高さまで。
掌は縦、指先は上に真っすぐ
息吹●吐
Stance ● Right Sanchin Dachi
Tech. ● Turn hands over into
Teisho Otoshi Uke
Point ● Blocks are in center of
left/right half of body, hand is at
elbow height. Fingers are facing
straight up
Ibuki ● To

立ち方●右三戦立ち
技●両掌を返して　鶴頭外受け
注意点●左右中心線を受け　肘の高
さ。掌を手首でなびかせ、肘は三戦
構え
息吹●呑
Stance ● Right Sanchin Dachi
Tech. ● Turn hands over from
the wrist into Kakuto Soto Uke
Point ● Blocks are in center of
left/right half of body at elbow
height. Elbow position is same
as Sanchin No Kamae
Ibuki ● Don

立ち方●右三戦立ち
技●両掌を返して　底掌内受け
注意点●左右中心線の位置まで。掌
は肘の高さ。掌を手首でなびかせ、
肘は三戦の構え
息吹●吐
Stance ● Right Sanchin Dachi
Tech. ● Turn hands over from
the wrist into Teisho Uchi Uke
Point ● Blocks stop at center
of left/right half of body. Elbow
position is same as Sanchin No
Kamae
Ibuki ● To

第32挙動

第33挙動

第34挙動

立ち方●右三戦立ち
技●両手を返してから　両手掬い受け
注意点●両肘を締める
息吹●呑
Stance ● Right Sanchin Dachi
Tech. ● Turn hands up into double arm Sukui Uke
Point ● Keep elbows close to body
Ibuki ● Don

立ち方●右三戦立ち
技●両手掌引き手
注意点●両肘を引いて掌は下向き
息吹●第32挙動から続けて呑
Stance ● Right Sanchin Dachi
Tech. ● Double arm Hikite
Point ● Pull both elbows back. Palms facing down
Ibuki ● Continue Don (from32)

立ち方●右三戦立ち
技●両手開手張り突き　両手貫手
息吹●吐
Stance ● Right Sanchin Dachi
Tech. ● Double arm Harizuki into double arm Nukite
Ibuki ● To

第 35 挙動	第 36 挙動	第 37 挙動

中間動作

裏側

立ち方●左三戦立ち
技●両手を返してから両手掬い受け
注意点●一歩下がる。両肘を締める。
息吹●呑
Stance ● Left Sanchin Dachi
Tech. ● Turn hands over into
double arm Sukui Uke from below
Point ● Step back w/ right foot.
Keep elbows close to body
Ibuki ● Don

立ち方●左三戦立ち
技●両手掌引き手
注意点●両肘を引いて掌は下向き
息吹●第35挙動から続けて呑
Stance ● Left Sanchin Dachi
Tech. ● Double arm Hikite
Point ● Pull elbows back. Palms
facing down
Ibuki ● Continue Don (from 35)

立ち方●左三戦立ち
技●両手開手張り突き　両手貫手
息吹●吐
Stance ● Left Sanchin Dachi
Tech. ● Double arm Harizuki into
double arm Nukite
Ibuki ● To

第38挙動　　　第39挙動　　　第40挙動

立ち方●右三戦立ち
技●両手を返し下から両手掬い受け
注意点●一歩後退。両肘を締める。
息吹●呑
Stance ● Right Sanchin Dachi
Tech. ● Turn hands over into
double arm Sukui Uke from below
Point ● Step back w/ left foot.
Keep elbows close to body
Ibuki ● Don

立ち方●右三戦立ち
技●両手掌引き手
注意点●両肘を引いて掌は下向き
息吹●第38挙動から続けて呑
Stance ● Right Sanchin Dachi
Tech. ● Double arm Hikite
Point ● Pull elbows back. Palms
facing down
Ibuki ● Continue Don (from 38)

立ち方●右三戦立ち
技●両手開手張り突き
息吹●吐
Stance ● Right Sanchin Dachi
Tech. ● Double arm Harizuki (
open hands)
Ibuki ● To

第41挙動　　　第42挙動

中間動作

裏側

立ち方●左三戦立ち
技●右廻し受け　両手掌引き手
注意点●右足一歩後退
息吹●呑
Stance ● Left Sanchin Dachi
Tech. ● Mawashiuke right hand
on top into double Hikite
Point ● Step back w/ right foot
Ibuki ● Don

立ち方●左三戦立ち
技●両手底掌当て
息吹●吐
Stance ● Left Sanchin Dachi
Tech. ● Double arm Teisho Ate (
right hand on top)
Ibuki ● To

第43挙動　　　第44挙動

立ち方●右三戦立ち
技●左廻し受け　両手掌引き手
注意点●左足一歩後退
息吹●呑
Stance ● Right Sanchin Dachi
Tech. ● Mawashiuke left hand
on top into double Hikite
Point ● Step back w/ left foot
Ibuki ● Don

立ち方●右三戦立ち
技●左廻し受け　両手底掌当て
息吹●吐
Stance ● Right Sanchin Dachi
Tech. ● Double arm Teisho Ate (
left hand on top)
Ibuki ● To

直って	直って	気を付け

中間動作

裏側

立ち方●前足を引いて結び立ち
技●右手掌上に重ねる
息吹●呑
Stance ● Step back w/ right foot into Musubidachi
Tech. ● Place right hand on top of left
Ibuki ● Don (Inhale)

立ち方●結び立ち
技●手掌を摺り合わせて丹田集中
息吹●吐
Stance ● Musubidachi
Tech. ● Bring hands down in front of Tanden
Ibuki ● To (Exhale)

立ち方●結び立ち
注意点●顎を引き、両手は真っすぐ伸ばして大腿側部に付ける
Stance ● Musubidachi
Point ● Pull chin back. Keep fingers straight and hands on outer thight

礼　　　　　気を付け

立ち方●結び立ち
注意点●前方 30 度位、礼は深すぎ
ない
Stance ● Musubidachi
Point ● Bow forward for 30° .Be
careful not to bow too deeply

立ち方●結び立ち
注意点●顎を引き、両手は真っすぐ
伸ばして大腿側部に付ける
Stance ● Musubidachi
Point ● Pull chin back. Keep
fingers straight and hands on
outer thight

セイサン

十三手
Seisan

型のポイント

　「三戦」による三歩前進による突き、受けはサンセールではゆっくり行い、セイサンでは速く行う。演武線は四方向と単純で、それ程長い型ではないが、演武線前後左右の攻防は全て異なる技で構成され、四方向への攻防は、アンバランスを大きな特徴としている。

　剛柔流独特の接近戦による難度の高い技が連続している。それゆえ、この型の技術評価は厳しい。

　分解動作は、全日本空手道剛柔会が制定しているセイサン型分解組手（１本〜６本）から、一本目、二本目、三本目の一部を収録している。

The opening movements in Sanchin Dachi are the same as those performed in Sanseiru, however, they are performed quickly rather than slowly.

Seisan is performed in four directions but is simple and not very long. However, the attacks and blocks performed are different in each direction. It is said that the biggest point of this kata is that it is unbalanced.

The degree of difficulty of Goju-ryu's typical techniques in infighting is quite high. Because of that, people who perform Seisan as their best kata are more strictly criticized on those techniques.

The Seisan Kata Bunkai created by J.K.G.A. contains 6 parts all together. Pictures taken from parts 1, 2, and 3 are included in the following pages.

気を付け　礼　気を付け

中間動作

裏側

立ち方●結び立ち
注意点●顎を引き、両手は真っすぐ
伸ばして大腿側部につける
Stance ● Musubidachi
Point ● Pull chin back. Keep
fingers straight and hands on
outer thight

立ち方●結び立ち
注意点●前方30度位、礼は深すぎ
ない
Stance ● Musubidachi
Point ● Bow forward for 30° .Be
careful not to bow too deeply

立ち方●結び立ち
Stance ● Musubidachi

用意1

用意2

用意3

立ち方●結び立ち
注意点●右掌内側、丹田の前で重ね
集中
息吹●ゆっくり呑
Stance ● Musubidachi
Point ● Right hand on the inside.
Hands are crossed in front of
Tanden
Ibuki ● Inhale slowly

立ち方●平行立ち
注意点●爪先を支点に踵を外に開く
Stance ● Heiko Dachi
Point ● Keep balls of feet in
place and only move heels

立ち方●平行立ち
注意点●両拳は脇を締めながら体側
へ、正拳は真下へ向けて、両肩を落
とす
息吹●ゆっくり吐
Stance ● Heiko Dachi
Point ● Keep elbows against
side of body, fists pointing
straight down, and shoulders
relaxed
Ibuki ● Exhale slowly

第1挙動	第2挙動	第3挙動

中間動作

裏側

立ち方●右三戦立ち
技●三戦の構え、右拳外側より両手交差
注意点●右足を内側中心線より一歩前進。三戦の型と同じ
Stance ● Right Sanchin Dachi
Tech. ● Cross arms into San-chin No Kamae. Right arm is on the outside when making Kamae. Same as Sanchin Kata

立ち方●右三戦立ち
技●左拳　引き手
注意点●三戦の型と同じ
Stance ● Right Sanchin Dachi
Tech. ● Right Hikite
Point ● Same as Sanchin Kata

立ち方●右三戦立ち
技●左拳　正拳突き
注意点●三戦の型と同じ。突きは速く
Stance ● Right Sanchin Dachi
Tech. ● Left Hikite
Point ● Same as Sanchin Kata. Punch quickly

第４挙動

第５挙動

第６挙動

立ち方●右三戦立ち
技●左拳　中段横受け
注意点●三戦の型と同じ。第３挙動
から続ける。受けは速く
Stance ● Right Sanchin Dachi
Tech. ● Left Chudan Yoko Uke
Point ● Same as Sanchin Kata.
Do 3-4 quickly as one combination. Block quickly

立ち方●左三戦立ち
技●足だけ前進
注意点●三戦の型と同じ。上肢・下
肢の締め
Stance ● Left Sanchin Dachi
Tech. ● Step forward w/ left foot
Point ● Same as Sanchin Kata.
Tense arms and legs

立ち方●左三戦立ち
技●右拳　引き手
注意点●三戦の型と同じ
Stance ● Left Sanchin Dachi
Tech. ● Right Hikite
Point ● Same as Sanchin Kata

第7挙動	第8挙動	第9挙動

中間動作

裏側

立ち方●左三戦立ち
技●右拳　正拳突き
注意点●三戦の型と同じ。突きは速く
Stance ● Left Sanchin Dachi
Tech. ● Right Seiken Tsuki
Point ● Same as Sanchin Kata.
Punch quickly

立ち方●左三戦立ち
技●右拳　中段横受け
注意点●三戦の型と同じ。受けは速
く。第7挙動から続ける
Stance ● Left Sanchin Dachi
Tech. ● Right Chudan Yoko Uke
Point ● Same as Sanchin Kata.
Block quickly. Do 7-8 quickly as
one combination

立ち方●右三戦立ち
技●足だけ前進
注意点●三戦の型と同じ。上肢・下
肢の締め
Stance ● Right Sanchin Dachi
Tech. ● Step forward w/ right foot
Point ● Same as Sanchin Kata.
Tense arms and legs

一本目
No.1

第 10 挙動　　　　第 11 挙動　　　　第 12 挙動

立ち方●右三戦立ち
技●左拳　引き手
注意点●三戦の型と同じ
Stance ● Right Sanchin Dachi
Tech. ● Left Hikite
Point ● Same as Sanchin Kata

立ち方●右三戦立ち
技●左拳　正拳突き
注意点●三戦の型と同じ。突きは速く
Stance ● Right Sanchin Dachi
Tech. ● Left Seiken Tsuki
Point ● Same as Sanchin Kata.
Punch quickly

立ち方●右三戦立ち
技●左拳　中段横受け
注意点●三戦の型と同じ。第11挙動
から続ける。受けは速く
Stance ● Right Sanchin Dachi
Tech. ● Left Chudan Yoko Uke
Point ● Same as Sanchin Kata.
Do 11-12 as one combination.
Block quickly

第 13 挙動	第 14 挙動	第 15 挙動

中間動作

裏側

立ち方●右三戦立ち
技●右上段底掌当て目潰し、左手は開手水月
注意点●右手手刀当てから続ける
Stance ● Right Sanchin Dachi
Tech. ● Right Jodan Teisho ate into Metsubushi (Eye strike). Place left open hand in front of solar plexus
Point ● Do 13-14 as one combination

立ち方●右三戦立ち
技●左掌に右手刀当て
注意点●正中線。水月の位置
Stance ● Right Sanchin Dachi
Tech. ● Shuto Ate on left palm
Point ● Shuto ate is in front of solar plexus and center of body

立ち方●右三戦立ち
技●左上段底掌当て目潰し、右手は開手水月
Stance ● Right Sanchin Dachi
Tech. ● Left Jodan Teisho Ate into Metsubushi (Eye Strike). Place right open hand in front of solar plexus

一本目
（続き）

第16挙動　第17挙動　第18挙動

立ち方●右三戦立ち
技●右上段底掌当て目潰し、左手は開手水月
注意点●第15挙動から続ける
Stance ● Right Sanchin Dachi
Tech. ● Right Jodan Teisho Ate into Metsubushi (Eye strike).
Left open hand is in front of the solar plexus
Point ● Do 15-16 as one combination

立ち方●右三戦立ち
技●両手底掌押さえ
注意点●臍下丹田の位置
Stance ● Right Sanchin Dachi
Tech. ● Double hand Teisho Osae
Point ● Teisho Osae is in front of Tanden

立ち方●左足立ち
技●両手掬い受け
注意点●右足後方踵蹴り上げ
Stance ● Hidari Ashi Dachi (Stand on left foot)
Tech. ● Double arm Sukui Uke
Point ● Kick up w/ right heel to rear

第 19 挙動	第 20 挙動	第 21 挙動

裏側

立ち方●右足前摺り足立ち	立ち方●左足立ち	立ち方●右足前摺り足立ち
技●両手張り貫手突き	技●両手掬い受け	技●両手張り貫手突き
注意点●脇腹へ貫手突き	注意点●右足後方踵蹴り上げ	注意点●脇腹へ貫手突き
Stance ● Right Suriashi Dachi	Stance ● Hidari Ashi Dachi (Stand on left foot)	Stance ● Right Suriashi Dachi
Tech. ● Double arm Hari Nukite Tsuki	Tech. ● Double arm Sukui Uke	Tech. ● Double arm Hari Nukite Tsuki
Point ● Nukite Tsuki to opponent's side under ribs	Point ● Kick up w/ right heel to rear	Point ● Nukite Tsuki to opponent's side under ribs

第22挙動

第23挙動

第24挙動

立ち方●左足立ち
技●両手掬い受け
注意点●右足後方踵蹴り上げ
Stance ● Hidari Ashi Dachi
(Stand on left foot)
Tech. ● Double arm Sukui Uke
Point ● Kick up w/ right heel to
rear

立ち方●右足前摺り足立ち
技●両手張り貫手突き
注意点●脇腹へ貫手突き
Stance ● Right Suriashi Dachi
Tech. ● Double arm Hari Nukite
Tsuki
Point ● Nukite Tsuki to oppo-
nent's side under ribs

立ち方●右足前摺り足立ち
技●両手引き込み
注意点●三戦の両手引き込みと同じ
Stance ● Right Suriashi Dachi
Tech. ● Pull both arms
Point ● Same as Double Hikite
from Sanchin Kata

二本目
No.2

<table>
<tr>
<td align="center">第 25 挙動</td>
<td align="center">第 26 挙動</td>
<td align="center">第 27 挙動</td>
</tr>
<tr>
<td></td>
<td></td>
<td></td>
</tr>
</table>

中間動作

裏側

立ち方●右足膝上げ
技●両手引き込み
Stance ● Raise right knee
Tech. ● Pull both arms back

技●右関節蹴り、両手引き手
注意点●腰は入れ過ぎない
Tech. ● Right Kansetsu Keri.
Double arm Hikite
Point ● Don't twist hips too far

立ち方●右蹴り引き足
技●両手引き手
Stance ● Right Hikiashi (pull kicking leg back)
Tech. ● Double arm Hikite

【分解】
Bunkai

第 28 挙動	第 29 挙動	第 30 挙動

立ち方●左三戦立ち
技●両手掬い受け
注意点●左手上
Stance ● Left Sanchin Dachi
Tech. ● Double arm Sukui Uke
Point ● Left hand on top

立ち方●左三戦立ち
技●左掛け受け
注意点●第28挙動と繋げる
Stance ● Left Sanchin Dachi
Tech. ● Left Kakeuke
Point ● 28-29 are considered
one set of techniques

立ち方●右三戦立ち
技●両手掬い受け
注意点●右手上
Stance ● Right Sanchin Dachi
Tech. ● Double arm Sukui Uke
Point ● Right hand on top

第31挙動	第32挙動	第33挙動

中間動作

裏側

立ち方●右三戦立ち
技●右掛け受け
注意点●第30挙動と繋げる
Stance ● Right Sanchin Dachi
Tech. ● Right Kakeuke
Point ● 30-31 are considered one set of techniques

立ち方●左三戦立ち
技●両手掬い受け
注意点●左手上
Stance ● Left Sanchin Dachi
Tech. ● Double arm Sukui Uke
Point ● Left hand on top

立ち方●左三戦立ち
技●左掛け受け
Stance ● Left Sanchin Dachi
Tech. ● Left Kakeuke

【分解】
Bunkai

三本目　No.3

第 34 挙動　　第 35 挙動

立ち方●左三戦立ち
技●左手逆取り
注意点●第33挙動と繋げる
Stance ● Left Sanchin Dachi
Tech. ● Left Gyaku Tori
Point ● 33-34 are considered
one set of techniques

立ち方●右摺り足立ち
技●右腕受けから指鋏
注意点●右腕を絡ませ咽喉に指鋏突き・
絞り
Stance ● Right Suriashi Dachi
Tech. ● Right Ude Uke into Yubi
Basami
Point ● Twist right arm around
opponent's arm and perform Yubi
Basami Tsuki to throat and squeeze

立ち方●右摺り足立ち　そのまま
技●左正拳突き
Stance ● Right Suriashi Dachi
Tech. ● Left Seiken Tsuki

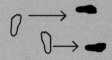

第 36 挙動	第 37 挙動	第 38 挙動

中間動作

裏側

立ち方●右摺り足立ち　そのまま
技●右正拳突き
注意点●第35挙動と繋げる
Stance ● Right Suriashi Dachi
Tech. ● Right Seiken Tsuki
Point ● Do 35-36 as one combination

立ち方●右摺り足立ち　そのまま
技●右止め受け
注意点●正拳の右脇、右肘を締める
Stance ● Right Suriashi Dachi
Tech. ● Right Tome Uke
Point ● Keep right elbow and arm close to body

立ち方●右足膝上げ
技●右止め受け
Stance ● Raise right knee
Tech. ● Right Tome Uke

第39挙動　　　第40挙動

技●右関節蹴り　右止め受け
注意点●腰は入れ過ぎない
Tech. ● Right Kansetsu Keri.
Right Tome Uke
Point ● Don't twist hips too far

立ち方●右蹴り引き足
技●右止め受け
Stance ● Right Hikiashi (pull
kicking leg back)
Tech. ● Right Tome Uke

第 41 挙動	第 42 挙動	第 43 挙動

中間動作

裏側

立ち方●左前屈立ち
技●前後底掌当て
注意点●真後ろに回り、右手中段底掌受け。左中段、右後方下段底掌当て
Stance ● Left Zenkutsu Dachi
Tech. ● Teisho Ate (front and rear)
Point ● Turn 180°, right Chudan Teisho Uke into double Teisho Ate (left hand Chudan, right hand Gedan)

立ち方●左四股立ち斜角
技●両手中段掛け受け
注意点●後足踵を送り込み、前進
Stance ● Left Shiko Dachi 45°
Tech. ● Double arm Chudan Kakeuke
Point ● Bring back heel parallel to front foot before stepping into Shiko Dachi

立ち方●左四股立ち斜角
技●右上段正拳突き
Stance ● Left Shiko Dachi 45°
Tech. ● Right Jodan Seiken Tsuki

第44挙動　　第45挙動　　第46挙動

立ち方●左四股立ち斜角
技●左中段正拳突き
Stance ● Left Shiko Dachi 45°
Tech. ● Left Chudan Seiken Tsuki

立ち方●左四股立ち斜角
技●右中段正拳突き
Stance ● Left Shiko Dachi 45°
Tech. ● Right Chudan Seiken Tsuki

立ち方●右四股立ち斜角
技●右中段止め受け
注意点●正拳の右脇、右肘を締める。第43挙動から連続
Stance ● Right Shiko Dachi 45°
Tech. ● Right Chudan Tome Uke
Point ● Keep right elbow and arm close to body. Do 43-46 as one combination

第 47 挙動	第 48 挙動	第 49 挙動

中間動作

裏側

立ち方●右足膝上げ
技●右中段止め受け
注意点●目線は北
Stance ● Raise right knee
Tech. ● Right Chudan Tome Uke
Point ● Look north

技●右中段足刀蹴り
注意点●上体は倒さない
Tech. ● Right Chudan Sokuto Keri
Point ● Keep body straight

立ち方●右蹴り引き足
技●左中段底掌落し受け、右手は上げ突き引き手
Stance ● Left Hikiashi (pull kicking leg back)
Tech. ● Left Chudan Teisho Otoshi Uke. Right hand is Hikite for Age Tsuki

第50挙動	第51挙動	第52挙動

立ち方●右四股立ち直角
技●右上げ突き、左手水月カバー
注意点●気合
Stance ● Right Shiko Dachi 90°
Tech. ● Right Age Tsuki. Left hand defends solar plexus
Point ● Kiai

立ち方●右四股立ち直角
技●右上段裏打ち、左手水月カバー
Stance ● Right Shiko Dachi 90°
Tech. ● Right Jodan Urauchi. Left hand defends solar plexus

立ち方●右四股立ち直角
技●右肘落し当て、左手水月カバー
Stance ● Right Shiko Dachi 90°
Tech. ● Right Hiji Otoshi Ate. Left hand defends solar plexus

第53挙動	第54挙動	第55挙動

中間動作

裏側

立ち方●右四股立ち直角
技●右下段払い、左手引き手
Stance ● Right Shiko Dachi 90°
Tech. ● Right Gedan Barai. Left
Hikite

立ち方●右四股立ち直角
技●左中段鈎突き、右手引き手
Stance ● Right Shiko Dachi 90°
Tech. ● Left Chudan Kagi Tsuki.
Right Hikite

立ち方●右猫足立ち
技●左中段鈎突き
注意点●腰を引き込み、体は北に向ける
Stance ● Right Nekoashi Dachi
Tech. ● Left Chudan Kagi Tsuki
Point ● Turn toward north after
pulling hips

第56挙動

第57挙動

第58挙動

立ち方●右足膝上げ
注意点●左右の拳はそのまま
Stance ● Raise right knee
Tech. ● Keep position of fists the same

技●右関節蹴り
注意点●腰を入れ過ぎない
Tech. ● Right Kansetsu Keri
Point ● Don't twist hips too far

立ち方●右蹴り引き足
注意点●左右の拳はそのまま
Stance ● Right Hikiashi (pull kicking leg back)
Point ● Keep fists position same

中間動作

裏側

立ち方●左三戦立ち
技●右内掛け受け
注意点●右足を交差、真後ろに回転
Stance ● Left Sanchin Dachi
Tech. ● Right Uchi Kakeuke
Point ● Cross right leg in front and turn 180°

立ち方●左三戦立ち
技●左外掛け受け
Stance ● Left Sanchin Dachi
Tech. ● Left Soto Kakeuke

立ち方●左三戦立ち
技●右外掛け受け
注意点●第59挙動から受けを繋げる。両手掛け受け三戦構えとなる
Stance ● Left Sanchin Dachi
Tech. ● Right Soto Kakeuke
Point ● 59-61 are considered one set of techniques. Make double arm Kakeuke Sanchin No Kamae

第62挙動　第63挙動

立ち方●左三戦立ち
技●両手引き手
注意点●両手を交差、肘から引き取る
Stance ● Left Sanchin Dachi
Tech. ● Double Hikite
Point ● When making Hikite, cross arms and pull back from elbows

技●右前蹴り、両手引き手
Tech. ● Right Maegeri, double Hikite

第64挙動

第65挙動

裏側

立ち方●左猫足立ち
技●右中段正拳突き、左手添え
注意点●左添え手は右正拳内腕。気合
Stance ● Left Nekoashi Dachi
Tech. ● Right Chudan Seiken
Tsuki. Keep left hand against
Point ● Place left hand on the
inside of right upper arm. Kiai

立ち方●左猫足立ち
技●右廻し受け
Stance ● Left Nekoashi Dachi
Tech. ● Mawashiuke right hand
on top

第66挙動 　　　直って 　　　直って

立ち方●左猫足立ち
技●両手底掌当て
Stance ● Left Nekoashi Dachi
Tech. ● Double arm Teisho Ate

立ち方●前足を引いて結び立ち
技●右手掌上に重ねる
息吹●呑
Stance ● Step back w/ right
foot into Musubidachi
Tech. ● Place right hand on top
of left
Ibuki ● Inhale

立ち方●結び立ち
技●手掌を摺り合わせて丹田集中
息吹●吐
Stance ● Musubidachi
Tech. ● Bring hands down in
front of Tanden
Ibuki ● Exhale

気を付け	礼	気を付け

中間動作

裏側

立ち方●結び立ち
注意点●顎を引き、両手は真っすぐ伸ばして大腿側部に付ける
Stance ● Musubidachi
Point ● Pull chin back. Keep fingers straight and hands on outer thight

立ち方●結び立ち
注意点●前方30度位、礼は深すぎない
Stance ● Musubidachi
Point ● Bow forward for 30°. Be careful not to bow too deeply

立ち方●結び立ち
注意点●顎を引き、両手は真っすぐ伸ばして大腿側部に付ける
Stance ● Musubidachi
Point ● Pull chin back. Keep fingers straight and hands on outer thight

シソーチン

四向鎮
Shisōchin

型のポイント

　「三戦」の三歩前進を開手にて行い、前屈立ちから後屈立ちへの腰の捻転による肘取り、前蹴りから前屈立ち肘当て等、大技による八方向への演武線が特徴である。
　左右前後とバランスを重視した点では八方向へ演武する初めての型に相応しい。
　分解動作は、全日本空手道剛柔会が制定しているシソーチン型分解組手（１本〜５本）から、一本目、二本目、三本目、四本目、五本目までの一部を掲載している。

Stepping in Sanchin Dachi is performed three times with opened hands.
Shishōchin is characterized by large, bold movements performed in eight directions such as Hiji Tori (breaking opponent's elbow) performed while changing from Zenkutsu Dachi to Kokutsu Dachi using hips, as well as Zenkutsu Dachi Hijiate performed after Maegeri. This kata is the first to demonstrate balanced movement in eight directions.
The Shisōchin Kata Bunkai created by J.K.G.A. contains 5 parts all together. Pictures taken from parts 1, 2, 3, 4, and 5 are included in the following pages.

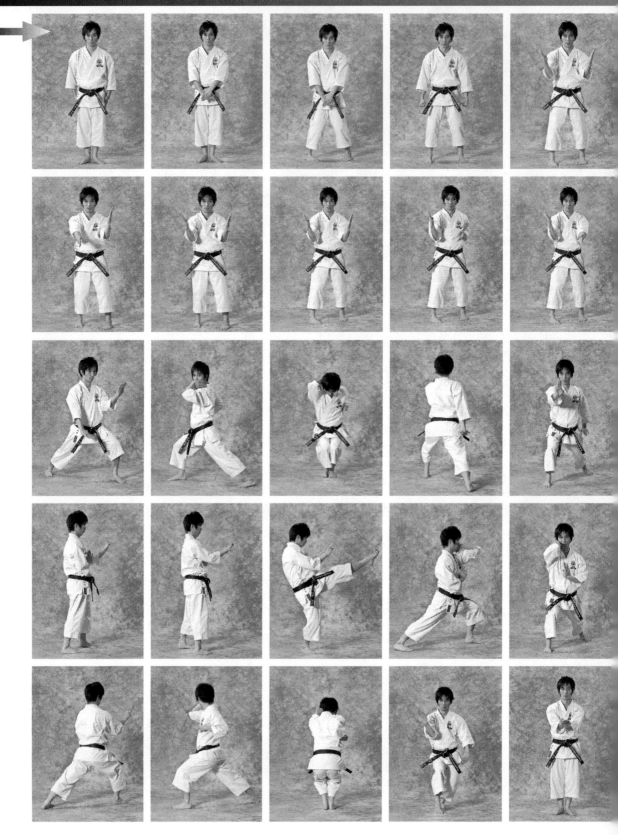

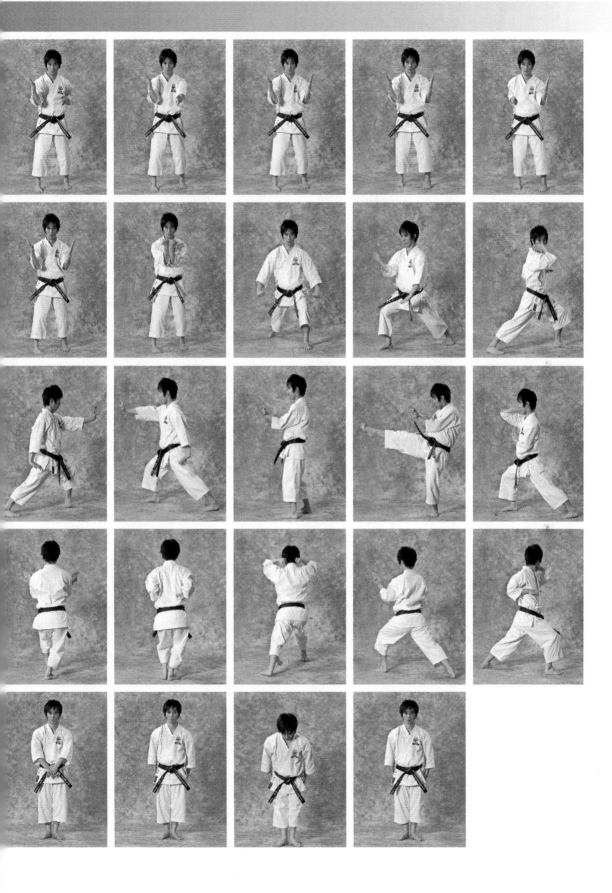

気を付け	礼	気を付け

中間動作

裏側

立ち方●結び立ち
注意点●顎を引き、両手は真っすぐ
伸ばして大腿側部につける
Stance ● Musubidachi
Point ● Pull chin back. Keep
fingers straight and hands on
outer thight

立ち方●結び立ち
注意点●前方 30 度位、礼は深すぎ
ない
Stance ● Musubidachi
Point ● Bow forward for 30° .Be
careful not to bow too deeply

立ち方●結び立ち
Stance ● Musubidachi

用意 1

用意 2

用意 3

立ち方●結び立ち
注意点●右掌内側、丹田の前で重ね集中
息吹●ゆっくり呑
Stance ● Musubidachi
Point ● Right hand on the inside. Hands are crossed in front of Tanden
Ibuki ● Inhale slowly

立ち方●平行立ち
注意点●爪先を支点に踵を外に開く
Stance ● Heiko Dachi
Point ● Keep balls of feet in place and only move heels

立ち方●平行立ち
注意点●両拳は脇を締めながら体側へ、正拳は真下へ向けて、両肩を落とす
息吹●ゆっくり吐
Stance ● Heiko Dachi
Point ● Keep elbows against side of body, fists pointing straight down, and shoulders relaxed
Ibuki ● Exhale slowly

第1挙動	第2挙動	第3挙動

裏側

立ち方●右三戦立ち
技●三戦構え、開手　右掌外側より
両手交差
注意点●右足を内側中心線より一歩
前進。三戦の型と同じ
Stance ● Right Sanchin Dachi
Tech. ● Cross arms into Sanchin
No Kamae (open hands). Right
arm is on the outside
Point ● Step forward w/ right
foot using an inward curve as
same as Sanchin Kata

立ち方●右三戦立ち
技●左掌　引き手
注意点●開手のまま引き手
Stance ● Right Sanchin Dachi
Tech. ● Left Hikite
Point ● Keep hands open

立ち方●右三戦立ち
技●左貫手突き
注意点●指先を伸ばし決めの時に手
首を締める
Stance ● Right Sanchin Dachi
Tech. ● Left Nukite Tsuki
Point ● Extend fingers and
tense the left wrist when using
Kime

【分解】
Bunkai

一本目　No.1

第４挙動　　　　第５挙動　　　　第６挙動

立ち方●右三戦立ち
技●左中段開手横受け
注意点●開手のまま背手で横受け
Stance ● Right Sanchin Dachi
Tech. ● Left Chudan Yoko Uke
(open hand)
Point ● Keep left hand open.
Yoko Uke w/ the back of hand

立ち方●左三戦立ち
技●足だけ前進
注意点●開手、三戦と同じ。上肢・
下肢の締め
Stance ● Left Sanchin Dachi
Tech. ● Step forwad w/ left foot
Point ● Keep hands open. Same
as Sanchin Kata. Keep arms
and legs tense

立ち方●左三戦立ち
技●右掌　引き手
注意点●開手のまま引き手
Stance ● Left Sanchin Dachi
Tech. ● Right Hikite
Point ● Keep hands open

第7挙動	第8挙動	第9挙動

中間動作

裏側

立ち方●左三戦立ち
技●右貫手突き
注意点●指先を伸ばし決めの時に手首を締める
Stance ● Left Sanchin Dachi
Tech. ● Right Nukite Tsuki
Point ● Extend fingers and tense the right wrist when using Kime

立ち方●左三戦立ち
技●右中段開手横受け
注意点●開手のまま背手で横受け
Stance ● Left Sanchin Dachi
Tech. ● Right Chudan Yoko Uke (open hand)
Point ● Keep right hand open. Yoko Uke w/ the back of hand

立ち方●右三戦立ち
技●足だけ前進
注意点●開手、三戦と同じ。上肢・下肢の締め
Stance ● Right Sanchin Dachi
Tech. ● Step forwad w/ right foot
Point ● Keep hands open. Same as Sanchin Kata. Keep arms and legs tense

第10挙動　　　　第11挙動　　　　第12挙動

立ち方●右三戦立ち
技●左掌　引き手
注意点●開手のまま引き手
Stance ● Right Sanchin Dachi
Tech. ● Left Hikite
Point ● Keep hands open

立ち方●右三戦立ち
技●左貫手突き
注意点●指先を伸ばし決めの時に手首を締める
Stance ● Right Sanchin Dachi
Tech. ● Left Nukite Tsuki
Point ● Extend fingers and tense the left wrist when using Kime

立ち方●右三戦立ち
技●左中段開手横受け
注意点●開手のまま背手で横受け
Stance ● Right Sanchin Dachi
Tech. ● Left Chudan Yoko Uke (open hand)
Point ● Keep left hand open. Yoko Uke w/ the back of hand

第13挙動　第14挙動

中間動作

裏側

立ち方●右三戦立ち
技●両手掬い受けから両拳に握る
注意点●正中線中段に両手を合わせる
Stance ● Right Sanchin Dachi
Tech. ● Double hand Sukui Uke into fists
Point ● Hands are in the center of the body and Chudan height while Sukui Uke

立ち方●前足を後ろに引いて左前屈立ち
技●両手拳　下段払い
注意点●右足を後方に下げると同時に払う
Stance ● Step back w/ front leg into left Zenkutsu Dachi
Tech. ● Gedan Barai w/ both fists
Point ● Step back w/ right foot at the same time as Gedan Barai

【分解】
Bunkai

一本目（続き）

第15挙動

立ち方●右前屈立ち
技●両手開手、右横受け左下払い
注意点●南西側に右足を前進
Stance ● Right Zenkutsu Dachi
Tech. ● Right Yoko Uke, left Shita Barai (open hands)
Point ● Step right foot southwest

第16挙動

立ち方●右後屈立ち
技●左手掛取り、右手肘当て（腕折）
注意点●腕関節を下から当て折り、目線は南。第15～16挙動は続ける
Stance ● Right Kokutsu Dachi
Tech. ● Left Kake Tori, Right Hijiate (break arm)
Point ● Hit joint of opponent's arm from below to break. Look south. Do 15-16 as one combination

二本目　No.2

第17挙動

第18挙動

中間動作

裏側

立ち方●左前屈立ち
技●両手開手、左横受け右下払い
注意点●南東側に左足を前進
Stance ● Left Zenkutsu Dachi
Tech. ● Left Yoko Uke, right Shita
Barai (open hands)
Point ● Step left foot southeast

立ち方●左後屈立ち
技●右手掛取り、左手肘当て（腕折）
注意点●腕関節を下から当て折り、目線は南。第17～18挙動は続ける
Stance ● Left Kokutsu Dachi
Tech. ● Right Kake Tori, left Hijiate (break arm)
Point ● Hit joint of opponent's arm from below to break. Look south. Do 17-18 as one combination

【分解】
Bunkai

二本目（続き）

第 19 挙動　　　　　　　　　　　　　　第 20 挙動

立ち方●左足を寄せて閉足立ち
技●右手後方正拳突き、左手後方肘当て
注意点●両膝を曲げて上体を前傾。目線下前方
Stance ● Heisoku Dachi
Tech. ● Right Seiken Tsuki, left Hijiate (both to rear)
Point ● Bend knees and lean body forward.Look down and forward

立ち方●左前屈立ち
技●両手底掌当て前後
注意点●右足を前方で交差、真後ろ北側に回転。動作はゆっくり
Stance ● Left Zenkutsu Dachi
Tech. ● Double hand Teisho Ate (front/rear)
Point ● Cross right leg in front of supporting leg and turn 180°. Do slowly

第21挙動 　　 第22挙動

中間動作

裏側

立ち方●右前屈立ち
技●両手底掌当て前後
注意点●左足を前方で交差、真後ろ南側に回転。動作
はゆっくり
Stance ● Right Zenkutsu Dachi
Tech. ● Double hand Teisho Ate (front/rear)
Point ● Cross left leg in front of supporting leg
and turn 180°. Do slowly

立ち方●左前屈立ち
技●両手底掌当て前後
注意点●左足を前方で交差、東側に転身。
動作はゆっくり
Stance ● Left Zenkutsu Dachi
Tech. ● Double hand Teisho Ate (front/rear)
Point ● Cross left leg in front of supporting leg and turn to the east. Do slowly

【分解】
Bunkai

三本目　No.3

第23挙動 第24挙動

立ち方●右前屈立ち
技●両手底掌当て前後
注意点●左足を前方で交差、真後ろ西側に回転。動作
はゆっくり
Stance ● Right Zenkutsu Dachi
Tech. ● Double hand Teisho Ate (front/rear)
Point ● Cross left leg in front of supporting leg
and turn 180°. Do slowly

立ち方●左三戦立ち
技●左掛け受け
注意点●動作はゆっくり
Stance ● Left Sanchin Dachi
Tech. ● Left Kakeuke
Point ● Do slowly

第 25 挙動　　第 26 挙動　　　第 27 挙動

裏側

技●右前蹴り
Tech. ● Right Maegeri

立ち方●右前屈立ち
技●右中段肘当て
注意点●第 25〜26 挙動は続ける。気合
Stance ● Right Zenkutsu Dachi
Tech. ● Right Chudan Hijiate
Point ● 25-26 are done as one
combination. Kiai

立ち方●左三戦立ち
技●左掛け受け
注意点●真後ろ東側に回転。動作はゆっ
くり
Stance ● Left Sanchin Dachi
Tech. ● Left Kakeuke
Point ● Turn 180˚ .Do slowly

第28挙動　　　第29挙動　　　第30挙動

立ち方●右三戦立ち
技●右掛け受け
注意点●動作はゆっくり
Stance ● Right Sanchin Dachi
Tech. ● Right Kakeuke
Point ● Do slowly

技●左前蹴り
Tech. ● Left Maegeri

立ち方●左前屈立ち
技●左中段肘当て
注意点●第29〜30挙動は続ける。気合
Stance ● Left Zenkutsu Dachi
Tech. ● Left Chudan Hijiate
Point ● 29-30 are done as one
combination. Kiai

四本目　No.4

第31挙動	第32挙動	第33挙動

裏側

立ち方●右前屈立ち
技●右中段肘当て
注意点●左足を北側へ引き南に転身
Stance ● Right Zenkutsu Dachi
Tech. ● Right Chudan Hijiate
Point ● Pull left foot towards the
north and turn to the south

立ち方●左猫足立ち
技●三戦開手構え
注意点●左足を引きつけ、真後ろ北側に回転
Stance ● Left Nekoashi Dachi
Tech. ● Sanchin No Kamae (open
hands)
Point ● Pull left foot in and turn 180°

【分解】
Bunkai

四本目（続き）

第34挙動　　　第35挙動

立ち方●右前屈立ち
技●両手後方正拳突き
注意点●開手三戦構えから拳を握り、体を前傾しながら後方両手突き
Stance ● Right Zenkutsu Dachi
Tech. ● Double Seiken Tsuki (rear)
Point ● Make fists from Sanchin No Kamae. Morote Tsuki to the rear while leaning body forward

立ち方●左前屈立ち
技●両手開手、左横受け右下払い
注意点●北西側に左足を前進
Stance ● Left Zenkutsu Dachi
Tech. ● Left Yoko Uke, right Shita Barai (open hands)
Point ● Step forward and northwest w/ left foot

第36挙動　　第37挙動

中間動作

裏側

立ち方●左後屈立ち
技●右手掛取り、左手肘当て（腕折）
注意点●腕関節を下から当て折り、目線
は北。第35～36挙動は続ける
Stance ● Left Kokutsu Dachi
Tech. ● Right Kake Tori, left Hijiate (
break arm)
Point ● Hit joint of opponent's arm
from below to break looking north.
Do 35-36 as one combination

立ち方●右前屈立ち
技●両手開手、右横受け左下払い
注意点●北東側に右足を前進
Stance ● Right Zenkutsu Dachi
Tech. ● Right Yoko Uke. Left Shita
Barai (open hands)
Point ● Step forward and northeast
w/ right foot

【分解】
Bunkai

五本目　No.5

第38挙動　　　第39挙動　　　第40挙動

立ち方●右後屈立ち
技●左手掛取り、右手肘当て（腕折）
注意点●腕関節を下から当て折り、第37～38挙動は続ける。目線は北。
Stance ● Right Kokutsu Dachi
Tech. ● Left Kake Tori, right Hijiate (break arm)
Point ● Hit joint of opponent's arm from below to break looking north. Do 37-38 as one combination.

立ち方●右足を寄せて閉足立ち
技●左手後方正拳突き、右手後方肘当て
注意点●両膝を曲げて上体を前傾。目線下前方
Stance ● Heisoku Dachi
Tech. ● Left Seiken Tsuki, right Hijiate (both to the rear)
Point ● Bend knees and lean body forward. Look down and forwad

立ち方●右猫足立ち
技●両手開手右横受け、左下払い
注意点●右回転。正面南に猫足立ち
Stance ● Right Nekoashi Dachi
Tech. ● Right Yoko Uke, left Shita Barai (open hands)
Point ● Turn clockwise into Nekoashi Dachi to the front (south)

直って	直って	気を付け

中間動作

裏側

立ち方●前足を引いて結び立ち
技●右手掌上に重ねる
息吹●呑
Stance ● Step back w/ right
foot into Musubidachi
Tech. ● Place right hand on top
of left
Ibuki ● Inhale

立ち方●結び立ち
技●手掌を摺り合わせて丹田集中
息吹●吐
Stance ● Musubidachi
Tech. ● Bring hands down in
front of Tanden
Ibuki ● Exhale

立ち方●結び立ち
注意点●顎を引き、両手は真っすぐ
伸ばして大腿側部に付ける
Stance ● Musubidachi
Point ● Pull chin back. Keep
fingers straight and hands on
outer thight

礼　　　　　　　　気を付け

立ち方●結び立ち
注意点●前方 30 度位、礼は深すぎ
ない
Stance ● Musubidachi
Point ● Bow forward for 30° .Be
careful not to bow too deeply

立ち方●結び立ち
注意点●顎を引き、両手は真っすぐ
伸ばして大腿側部に付ける
Stance ● Musubidachi
Point ● Pull chin back. Keep
fingers straight and hands on
outer thight

セーパイ

十八手
Seipai

型のポイント

　六方向、左右対称の演武線を持つセーパイは曲線重視の技法に合わせて体の転身も円運動を描き、連続技、逆手、倒し等多種多様な立ち方、攻防による変化に富んだ型である。全日本空手道剛柔会ではクルルンファーの前に位置し、当初は３段に合格しないと教授されない型であった。

　演武においては緩やかな円動作と鞭のようなしなり、微妙な腰の使い方、丹田集中のみならず、重心を落とした決め等留意点が多い型である。

　打ち、当て、突き、蹴り、倒し、投げ等、多彩な攻撃技と、中高一本拳、弾指打ち、熊手打ち等、特殊な手技が用いられている。

　分解動作は全日本空手道剛柔会が制定しているセーパイ型分解組手（１本〜５本）から、一本目、二本目、三本目、四本目、五本目の一部を掲載している。

Seipai is performed in six directions with left-right symmetry using many circular techniques.

It is full of a variety of techniques such as combinations, locks, sweeps, diverse stances, attack and blocks.

Formerly in Japan Karatedo Gojukai Association, Seipai was taught only at 3rd Dan and above, as it is the kata that comes before Kururunfa.

To properly demonstrate Seipai, it is required to use soft circular movements, whip-like movements, precise use of hips and concentration on Tanden.

Moreover, it has many small details to pay attention to such as Kime and keeping a low center of gravity.

Various attack techniques such as hitting, striking, punching, kicking, sweeping, and throwing, as well as special hand techniques such as Naka Taka Ipponken, Danshi Uchi, Kumade Uchi, etc. are included in Seipai.

The Seipai Kata Bunkai created by J.K.G.A. contains 5 parts all together. Pictures taken from 1, 2, 3, 4, and 5 are included in the following pages.

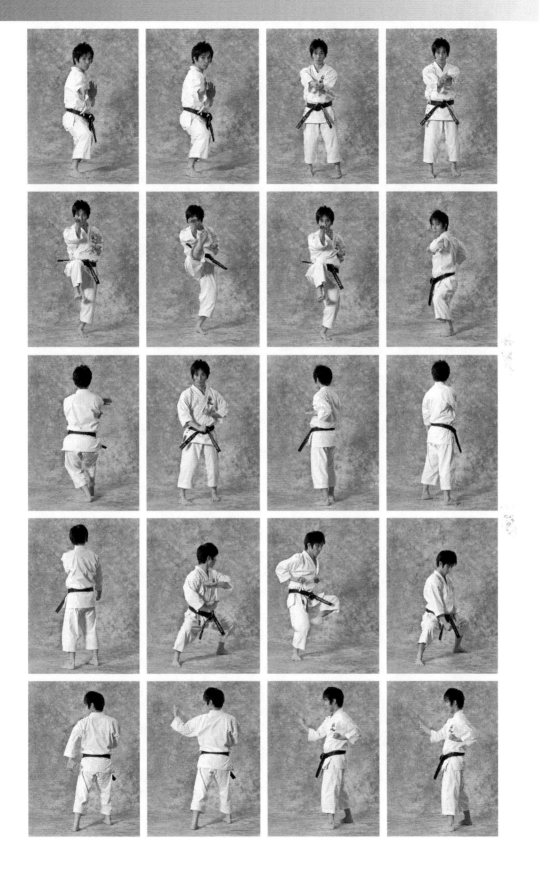

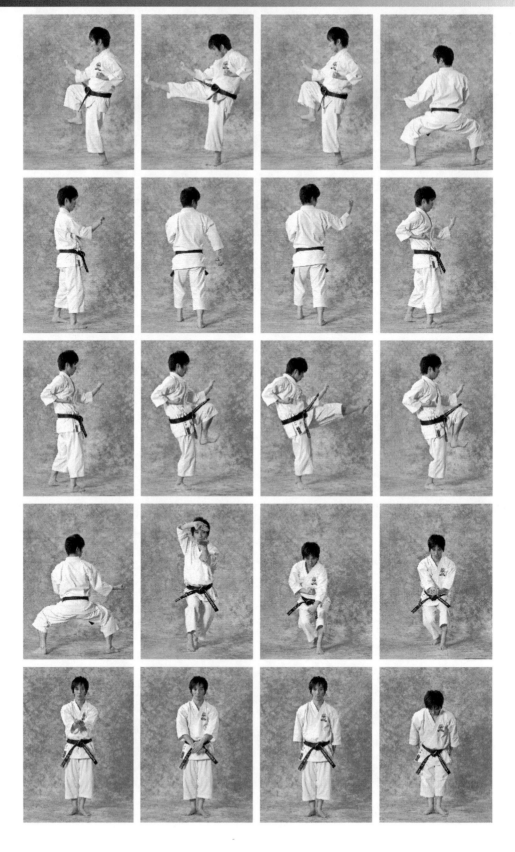

気を付け 　　 礼 　　 気を付け

立ち方●結び立ち
注意点●顎を引き、両手は真っすぐ
伸ばして大腿側部につける
Stance ● Musubidachi
Point ● Pull chin back. Keep
fingers straight and hands on
outer thight

立ち方●結び立ち
注意点●前方30度位、礼は深すぎ
ない
Stance ● Musubidachi
Point ● Bow forward for 30°. Be
careful not to bow too deeply

立ち方●結び立ち
Stance ● Musubidachi

用意1

用意2

用意3

中間動作

裏側

立ち方●結び立ち
注意点●右掌内側、丹田の前で重ね
集中
息吹●ゆっくり呑
Stance ● Musubidachi
Point ● Right hand on the inside.
Hands are crossed in front of
Tanden
Ibuki ● Inhale slowly

立ち方●平行立ち
注意点●爪先を支点に踵を外に開く
Stance ● Heiko Dachi
Point ● Keep balls of feet in
place and only move heels

立ち方●平行立ち
注意点●両拳は脇を締めながら体側
へ、正拳は真下へ向けて、両肩を落
とす
息吹●ゆっくり吐
Stance ● Heiko Dachi
Point ● Keep elbows against
side of body, fists pointing
straight down, and shoulders
relaxed
Ibuki ● Exhale slowly

第１挙動　　　第２挙動

立ち方●右四股立ち直角
技●左底掌受け
注意点●左足後退。受け手外側、右手内側
Stance ● Right Shiko Dachi 90°
Tech. ● Left Teisho Uke
Point ● Step back w/ left foot into
Shiko Dachi 90° . Blocking hand is
outside, right hand is inside

立ち方●右四股立ち直角
技●右貫手突き
注意点●貫手突きの決めは手首を締
める
Stance ● Right Shiko Dachi 90°
Tech. ● Right Nukite Tsuki
Point ● Tense wrist when using
Kime in Nukite Tsuki

一本目　No.1

第３挙動	第４挙動	第５挙動

中間動作

裏側

立ち方●左三戦立ち
技●両掌を重ねて握る。左手下
注意点●左手肘から右手掌に合わせる
Stance ● Left Sanchin Dachi
Tech. ● Clasp hands w/ right on top
Point ● Keep left elbow against body as left hand comes up to right hand

立ち方●右摺り足立ち
技●両手回旋外し、添え突き（左手上）
注意点●右回旋で外し添え突き
Stance ● Right Suriashi Dachi
Tech. ● Double arm Hazushi (break grab) into Soe tsuki
Point ● Twist hands to the right when performing Hazushi, from there perform Soe Tsuki

立ち方●右四股立ち直角
技●右肘跳ね上げ外し
注意点●左足を後退直角四股立ち
Stance ● Right Shiko Dachi 90°
Tech. ● Break grab using right elbow
Point ● Step back w/ left foot into Shiko Dachi 90°

第６挙動	第７挙動	第８挙動

立ち方●左後屈立ち
技●右上段掛け取り、左下段底掌当て
注意点●第３〜６挙動は一連動作
Stance ● Left Kokutsu Dachi
Tech. ● Right Jodan Kake Tori, Left Gedan Teisho Ate
Point ● Do 3-6 as one combination

立ち方●左後屈立ち
技●左中段開手横受け、右手はそのまま
注意点●ゆっくり
Stance ● Left Kokutsu Dachi
Tech. ● Left Chudan Yoko Uke. Keep right Kake Tori
Point ● Do slowly

立ち方●左半前屈立ち
技●右手刀打ち、左手開手引き手
注意点●後屈立ちから半前屈立ちに腰入れ
Stance ● Left Han Zenkutsu Dachi
Tech. ● Right Shuto Uchi, Left Hikite (open hand)
Point ● Change stance from Kokutsu Dachi into Han Zenkutsu Dachi using hips

一本目（続き）

第9挙動	第10挙動	第11挙動

裏側

技●右前蹴り
注意点●右手刀打ち、引き手がブレないように
Tech. ● Right Maegeri
Point ● Do not to move right Shuto Uchi and Hikite when Kicking

立ち方●左四股立ち直角
技●左横肘当て
注意点●右手は拳にて引き手
Stance ● Left Shiko Dachi 90°
Tech. ● Left Yoko Hijiate
Point ● Hikite w/ right fist

立ち方●左四股立ち直角
技●左上段裏打ち
注意点●左横肘当て、左上段裏打ちは続ける
Stance ● Left Shiko Dachi 90°
Tech. ● Left Jodan Urauchi
Point ● Do 10-11 as one combination

第12挙動	第13挙動	第14挙動

別角度

立ち方●左四股立ち直角
技●左下段払いおよび打ち
注意点●ゆっくり。第8～12挙動は一
連の動作
Stance ● Left Shiko Dachi 90°
Tech. ● Left Gedan Barai (It is also
used as Uchi)
Point ● Slowly. 8-12 are considered
one set of techniques

立ち方●右猫足立ち
技●右下段払い、左背手右肘支え
注意点●四股立ちの右足を引き寄せなが
ら。ゆっくり
Stance ● Right Nekoashi Dachi
Tech. ● Right Gedan Barai. Back of
left hand support right elbow
Point ● Pull right foot back. Slowly
from Shiko Dachi

立ち方●右猫足立ち
技●右中段受け
注意点●ゆっくり
Stance ● Right Nekoashi Dachi
Tech. ● Right Chudan Uke
Point ● Block slowly

一本目（続き）

二本目　No.2

第 15 挙動

第 16 挙動

中間動作

裏側

立ち方●右猫足立ち
技●右掛け受け
注意点●第13〜15挙動は一連動作。
ゆっくり
Stance ● Right Nekoashi Dachi
Tech. ● Right Kakeuke
Point ● 13-15 are considered one
set of techniques. Do slowly

立ち方●右三戦立ち
技●掛け取り腕巻き込み。腕折り下
段落とし
注意点●腕取り、右回転で腕折り。
脇と肘を締め、回転の折、軸のブレ
に注意
Stance ● Right Sanchin Dachi
Tech. ● Kake Tori, trap
opponent's arm. Break arm w/
Gedan Otoshi
Point ● After grabbing arm,
twist clockwise while trapping
arm (Keep arms close to body
during movement). Keep body
straight when turning

別角度

立ち方●右摺り足立ち
技●左掌を肘から顔の前で円を描くように廻し、再度引き手に取る。右手下段弾指打ち
注意点●体の回転に合わせて左肘外し、北西に摺り足で前進、右弾指打ち。弾指打ち
は手首のスナップで下から金的をはねる
Stance ● Right Suriashi Dachi
Tech. ● Using elbow, bring left palm across front of face and circle into Hikite. Right hand Gedan Danchi Uchi
Point ● While turning body, clear opponent's arm using left hand. Turn northwest and step forward into Suriashi dachi while performing Right Gedan Danchi Uchi.

立ち方●左摺り平行立ち
技●両手底掌押し
注意点●左手下段、右手上段を底掌押し
Stance ● Left Suri Heiko Dachi
Tech. ● Double arm Teisho Oshi
Point ● Left hand Gedan, right hand Jodan

二本目（続き）

第 19 挙動	第 20 挙動	第 21 挙動

裏側

立ち方●右四股立ち直角
技●両手掌を水月前で合わせる
注意点●目線は北西。両掌は肘から合わせ正中線で止める。両掌の間隔は頭一個分
Stance ● Right Shiko Dachi 90°
Tech. ● Place right hand above left in front of solar plexus
Point ● Look northwest. Palms stops in center of body. Distance between hands is as well as opponent's head

立ち方●右四股立ち直角
技●右足払い、両手引き手。
注意点●目線は北西から南西へ
Stance ● Right Shiko Dachi 90°
Tech. ● Right Ashibarai. Hikite w/ both hands
Point ● Look northwest and then southwest

立ち方●右四股立ち直角、腰落とし
技●両手中高一本拳突き
注意点●（昔は頭髪と顎鬚を掴んで首折り）足払いで倒して咽喉・水月に両手突き落とし。気合
Stance ● Right Shiko Dachi 90° (lower)
Tech. ● Double Naka Taka Ipponken Tsuki
Point ● Knock opponent down w/ Ashibarai. Tsuki Otoshi to throat and solar plexus. Kiai

第 22 挙動　　　第 23 挙動　　　第 24 挙動

立ち方●左四股立ち直角
技●左下段払い
注意点●四股立ちの直線後退は速く。第
21～22挙動は連続動作
Stance ● Left Shiko Dachi 90°
Tech. ● Left Gedan Barai
Point ● Step back quickly into Shiko Dachi.Do 21-22 as one combination

立ち方●右摺り平行立ち
技●両手底掌押し
注意点●右手下段、左手上段を底掌押し
Stance ● Right Suri Heiko Dachi
Tech. ● Double arm Teisho Oshi
Point ● Right hand Gedan, left hand Jodan

立ち方●左四股立ち直角
技●両手掌を水月前で合わせる
注意点●目線は北東。両掌は肘から合わせ正中線
で止める。両掌の間隔は頭一個分
Stance ● Left Shiko Dachi 90°
Tech. ● Place left hand above right
Point ● Look northeast.Palms stops in center of body. Distance between hands is as well as opponent's head

三本目　No.3

第 25 挙動	第 26 挙動	第 27 挙動

中間動作

裏側

立ち方●左四股立ち直角
技●左足払い　両手引き手
注意点●目線は北東から南東へ
Stance ● Left Shiko Dachi 90°
Tech. ● Left Ashibarai
Point ● Look northeast and south-east

立ち方●左四股立ち直角、腰落とし
技●両手中高一本拳突き
注意点●（昔は頭髪と顎鬚を掴んで首折り）足払いで倒して咽喉・水月に両手突き落とし。気合
Stance ● Left Shiko Dachi 90° (lower)
Tech. ● Double Naka Taka Ipponken Tsuki
Point ● Knock opponent down w/ Ashi-barai. Tsuki Otoshi to throat and solar plexus. Kiai

立ち方●右四股立ち直角
技●右下段払い
注意点●四股立ちの直線後退は速く。第26〜27挙動は連続動作
Stance ● Right Shiko Dachi 90°
Tech. ● Right Gedan Barai
Point ● Step back quickly into Shiko Dach. Do 26-27 as one combinaton

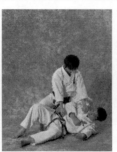

第28挙動	第29挙動	第30挙動

立ち方●左猫足立ち
技●左中段受け、右振り打ち
注意点●右足を北側へ移動。左足を寄せ
て猫足立ち。ゆっくり
Stance ● Left Nekoashi Dachi
Tech. ● Left Chudan Uke, right
Furiuchi
Point ● Move right foot toward north.
Pull left foot back into Nekoashi Dachi.
Slowly

立ち方●右弁足立ち
技●右中段受け、左振り打ち
注意点●右足から南側へ前進。左足は右足外側へ
交差させる。第28～29挙動は一連の動作
Stance ● Right Bensoku Dachi
Tech. ● Right Chudan Uke. Left Furiuchi
Point ● First move right foot towards
south. Cross left foot behind right. Do
28-29 as one combination

立ち方●左三戦立ち
技●左掛け受け、右手は水月
注意点●ゆっくり
Stance ● Left Sanchin Dachi
Tech. ● Left Kakeuke. Right hand in
front of solar plexus
Point ● Do slowly

四本目　No.4

第 31 挙動	第 32 挙動	第 33 挙動

中間動作

裏側

立ち方●半後屈立ち
技●左下段熊手打ち、右手は水月
注意点●三戦立ちから腰を切り返して打つ
Stance ● Han Kokutsu Dachi
Tech. ● Left Gedan Kumade Uchi.
Right hand is in front of solar plexus
Point ● From Sanchin Dachi twist hips while striking

立ち方●半後屈立ち
技●左上段裏打ち
注意点●第31～32挙動はスナップ動作で素早く
Stance ● Han Kokutsu Dachi
Tech. ● Left Jodan Urauchi
Point ● Do 31-32 quickly w/ snap

立ち方●左三戦立ち
技●右中段受け
注意点●半後屈立ちから腰を戻して中段受け。動作はゆっくり
Stance ● Left Sanchin Dachi
Tech. ● Right Chudan Uke
Point ● Rotate hips back from Han Kokutsu Dachi. Perform Chudan Uke Slowly.

第34挙動	第35挙動	第36挙動

立ち方●左三戦立ち
技●右掛け受け
注意点●受けた拳を掛け取り（腕取り）
Stance ● Left Sanchin Dachi
Tech. ● Right Kakeuke
Point ● Blocking arm performs Kake
Tori (Ude Tori)

技●右中段前蹴り
Tech. ● Right Chudan Maegeri

立ち方●左四股立ち直角
技●中高一本拳突き、右手掌は水月
注意点●第35～36挙動は連続
Stance ● Left Shiko Dachi 90°
Tech. ● Naka Taka Ipponken Tsuki.
Right palm is in front of solar plexus
Point ● Do 35-36 as one
combination

四本目（続き）

第 37 挙動　　　第 38 挙動　　　第 39 挙動

裏側

立ち方●右三戦立ち
技●右掛け受け、左手掌は水月
注意点●膝に重心を貯めてゆっくり転身
Stance ● Right Sanchin Dachi
Tech. ● Right Kakeuke. Put left
hand in front of solar plexus
Point ● Turn using knees slowly

立ち方●右半後屈立ち
技●右下段熊手打ち、左手掌は水月
注意点●三戦から腰を切り返して打つ
Stance ● Right Han Kokutsu Dachi
Tech. ● Right Gedan Kumade Uchi.
Left hand is in front of solar plexus
Point ● Hit using hips

立ち方●右半後屈立ち
技●右上段裏打ち
注意点●第 38 〜 39 挙動はスナップ動
作で素早く
Stance ● Right Han Kokutsu Dachi
Tech. ● Right Jodan Urauchi
Point ● Do 38-39 quickly w/ snap

【分解】
Bunkai

五本目　No.5

第40挙動　　　　第41挙動　　　　第42挙動

立ち方●右三戦立ち
技●左中段受け
注意点●半後屈立ちから腰を戻して中段
受け。動作はゆっくり
Stance ● Right Sanchin Dachi
Tech. ● Left Chudan Uke
Point ● Rotate hips back into
Chudan Uke slowly.

立ち方●右三戦立ち
技●左掛け受け
注意点●受けた拳を掛け取り（腕取り）
Stance ● Right Sanchin Dachi
Tech. ● Left Kakeuke
Point ● Blocking arm performs Kake
Tori (Ude Tori)

技●左前蹴り
Tech. ● Left Maegeri

五本目（続き）

第43挙動　　　　第44挙動　　　　第45挙動

裏側

別角度

立ち方●右四股立ち直角
技●中高一本拳突き、左手掌は水月
注意点●第42〜43挙動は連続
Stance ● Right Shiko Dachi 90°
Tech. ● Naka Taka Ipponken Tsuki.
Left palm is in front of solar plexus
Point ● Do 42-43 as one combi-naiton

立ち方●右猫足立ち
技●右開手上段受け、左開手肘取り
注意点●右足を一足引き右猫足立ちに
Stance ● Right Nekoashi Dachi
Tech. ● Right Jodan Uke, left Hiji Tori (open hands)
Point ● Pull right foot back into Nekoashi Dachi

立ち方●左猫足立ち
技●腕取りから前方へ捻転倒し
注意点●肘を支点に捩り倒す。目線は前方下
Stance ● Left Nekoashi dachi
Tech. ● Twist opponent and throw down
Point ● Throw using elbows. Look down and forward

第46挙動	直って	直って

立ち方●左猫足立ち
技●右下段鉄槌打ち、左開手側頭部押さえ
注意点●両手肘の円で打ち込み。目線は鉄槌拳を見る
Stance ● Left Nekoashi Dachi
Tech. ● Right Gedan Tettsui Uchi. Left Osae to side of head (open hand)
Point ● Elbows move in a circle when hitting. Look at Tettsui

立ち方●結び立ち
注意点●顎を引き、両手は真っすぐ伸ばして大腿側部に付ける
Stance ● Musubidachi
Point ● Pull chin back. Keep fingers straight and hands on outer thight

立ち方●結び立ち
注意点●前方30度位、礼は深すぎない
Stance ● Musubidachi
Point ● Bow forward for 30° .Be careful not to bow too deeply

五本目（続き）

気を付け　　　　　　　礼　　　　　　　気を付け

中間動作

裏側

立ち方●結び立ち
注意点●顎を引き、両手は真っすぐ
伸ばして大腿側部に付ける
Stance ● Musubidachi
Point ● Pull chin back. Keep
fingers straight and hands on
outer thight

立ち方●結び立ち
注意点●前方30度位、礼は深すぎ
ない
Stance ● Musubidachi
Point ● Bow forward for 30° .Be
careful not to bow too deeply

立ち方●結び立ち
注意点●顎を引き、両手は真っすぐ
伸ばして大腿側部に付ける
Stance ● Musubidachi
Point ● Pull chin back. Keep
fingers straight and hands on
outer thight

クルルンファー

久留頓破
Kururunfa

型のポイント

　八方向の演武線で左右のバランスを重視し、体の捌きは左右、前後に加えて腰の切り返しが剛柔流に相応しく、速攻と柔らかさの緩急が要求される。特に'引き'の動作には重厚な転身が求められる。

　後半の大の字からの'羽交い絞め外し'は大きな特徴で、型の分解の重要さを見せ付ける。上段の「交差受け」からの手掌の旋回は蓮の花の開花を表現したとも言われ、型に含まれる自然描写の美しさを思わせる。

　左右への繰り受けを猫足立ちで行う場合もあるが、本書は鷺足立ちで捌いて、すかさず関節蹴りを行う。繰り受けを受けとして使用する場合と、腕折りとして使用する場合を考慮して分解において左右異なる分解動作とした。

　分解動作は、全日本空手道剛柔会（１本～５本）が制定しているクルルンファー型分解組手から一本目、二本目、三本目、四本目、五本目の一部を掲載している。

Kururunfa is performed in eight directions and is balanced towards right and left. The various movements to the right, left, front and rear, as well as stance transitions using the hips capture the essence of Goju-ryu.

Quick attacks as well as softness are required. Also, Hiki (pulling techniques) requires solid and heavy movement when changing positions.

It is characterized at the latter part by Hagaijime Hazushi (to break out of a full nelson) from Dainoji Kamae, in which one stands extending both arms horizontally like the kanji character " 大 ". To correctly perform this technique is shown when attempting the importance of Bunkai.

Circling the hands after Jodan Kosa Uke is said to resemble a blooming lotus flower. We learn how the beauty of nature is used to describe kata.

Kuri Uke to left/right side can be performed in Nekoashi Dachi. In this manual, it is performed in Sagiashi Dachi to dodge opponent's attack and immediately kick with Kansetsu Keri.

Kuri Uke can be used either as a blocking or to break opponent's arm. According to that, different Bunkai is shown for the first one and second movement in this manual.

Kururunfa Kata Bunkai created by J.K.G.A. contains 5 parts all together. Pictures taken from parts 1, 2, 3, 4, and 5 are included in the following pages.

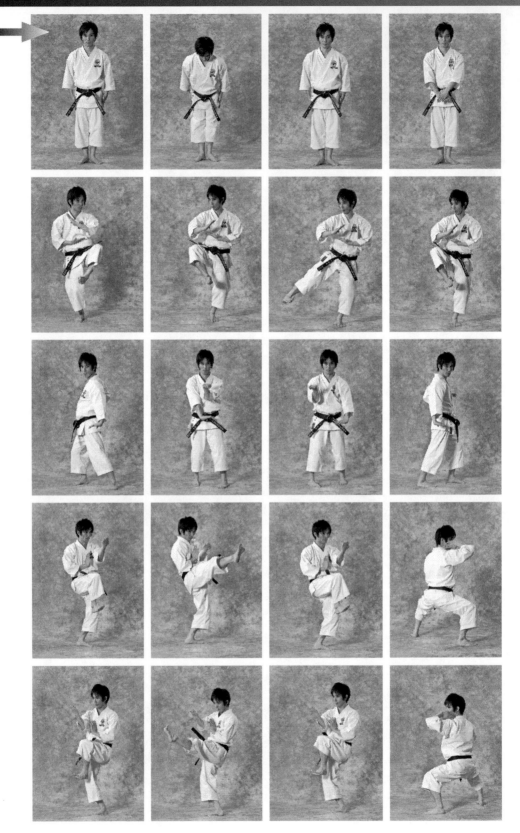

気を付け　　　　　　礼　　　　　　気を付け

中間動作

裏側

立ち方●結び立ち
注意点●顎を引き、両手は真っすぐ
伸ばして大腿側部につける
Stance ● Musubidachi
Point ● Pull chin back. Keep
fingers straight and hands on
outer thight

立ち方●結び立ち
注意点●前方30度位、礼は深すぎ
ない
Stance ● Musubidachi
Point ● Bow forward for 30°.Be
careful not to bow too deeply

立ち方●結び立ち
Stance ● Musubidachi

用意1

用意2

用意3

立ち方●結び立ち
注意点●右掌内側、丹田の前で重ね集中
息吹●ゆっくり呑
Stance ● Musubidachi
Point ● Right hand on the inside. Hands are crossed in front of Tanden
Ibuki ● Inhale slowly

立ち方●平行立ち
注意点●爪先を支点に踵を外に開く
Stance ● Heiko Dachi
Point ● Keep balls of feet in place and only move heels

立ち方●平行立ち
注意点●両拳は脇を締めながら体側へ、正拳は真下へ向けて、両肩を落とす
息吹●ゆっくり吐
Stance ● Heiko Dachi
Point ● Keep elbows against side of body. fists pointing straight down, and shoulders relaxed
Ibuki ● Exhale slowly

第１挙動　　第２挙動

中間動作

裏側

立ち方●右鷺足立ち
技●右開手内受け、左掌繰り受け
注意点●西に移動しながら鷺足と繰り受けが同時。ゆっくり。目線は南東
Stance ● Right Sagiashi Dachi
Tech. ● Right Uchi Uke (open hand), left Kuri Uke
Point ● Perform Sagiashi Dachi and block at the same time while moving west. Do slowly. Look southeast

技●左関節蹴り
注意点●関節蹴りは南東方向斜め
Tech. ● Left Kansetsu Keri
Point ● Kick toward southeast diagonally

【分解】
Bunkai

一本目　No.1

第３挙動

第４挙動

立ち方●左鷺足立ち
技●左開手内受け、右掌繰り受け
注意点●東に移動しながら鷺足と繰り受けが同時。ゆっくり。目線は南西
Stance ● Left Sagiashi Dachi
Tech. ● Left Uchi Uke (open hand), right Kuri Uke
Point ● Perform Sagiashi Dachi and block at the same time while moving east. Do slowly. Look southwest

技●左関節蹴り引き足
注意点●第１〜３挙動は一連動作
Tech. ● Hikiashi of Kansetsu Keri
Point ● 1-3 are considered one set of techniques

第5挙動	第6挙動	第7挙動

中間動作

裏側

立ち方●右三戦立ち
技●右掌掬い受け、左掌下段底掌落とし
注意点●右掌上（右中心線）、左掌（左中心線）。ゆっくり。三戦立ちと受けとを合わせる
Stance ● Right Sanchin Dachi
Tech. ● Right Sukui Uke, left Gedan Teisho Otoshi
Point ● Right hand on top. Blocks are in center of right/left half of body. Do slowly. Block while making Sanchin Dachi

技●右関節蹴り
注意点●関節蹴りは南西方向斜め
Tech. ● Right Kansetsu Keri
Point ● Kick towards southwest diagonally

技●右関節蹴り引き足
注意点●第4～6挙動は一連動作
Tech. ● Hikiashi of Kansetsu Keri
Point ● 4-6 are considered one set of techniques

【分解】
Bunkai

一本目（続き）

第8挙動　第9挙動　第10挙動

立ち方●右半後屈立ち
技●右掌下段払い、左掌引き手
注意点●三戦立ちから腰を切って半後屈立ち

Stance ● Right Han Kokutsu Dachi
Tech. ● Right Gedan Barai, Left Hikite
Point ● Change stance from Sanchin Dachi into Han Kokutsu Dachi using hips

立ち方●右三戦立ち
技●右掌掬い受け、左掌下段底掌落とし
注意点●正中線、右掌上・左掌下。第7〜9挙動は一連の動作。第8〜9挙動は連続で速く

Stance ● Right Sanchin Dachi
Tech. ● Right Sukui Uke, left Gedan Teisho Otoshi
Point ● Block is in center of body. Right hand on top. 7-9 are considered one set of techniques. Do 8-9 quickly as one combination

立ち方●左三戦立ち
技●左掌掬い受け、右掌下段底掌落とし
注意点●左掌上（左中心線）、右掌下（右中心線）。ゆっくり。前進と受けを合わせる

Stance ● Left Sanchin Dachi
Tech. ● Left Sukui Uke, right Gedan Teisho Otoshi
Point ● Left hand on top. Blocks are in center of right/left half of body. Block while stepping forward

第11挙動　　　　第12挙動　　　　第13挙動

中間動作

裏側

立ち方●左半後屈立ち
技●左掌下段払い、右掌引き手
注意点●三戦立ちから腰を切って半後屈立ち

Stance ● Left Han Kokutsu Dachi
Tech. ● Left Gedan Barai, right Hikite
Point ● Change stance from Sanchin Dachi into Han Kokutsu Dachi ushing hips

立ち方●左三戦立ち
技●左掌掬い受け、右掌下段底掌落とし
注意点●正中線、左掌上・右掌下。第10〜12挙動は一連の動作。第11〜12挙動は連続で

Stance ● Left Sanchin Dachi
Tech. ● Left Sukui Uke, right Gedan Teisho Otoshi
Point ● Blocks are in center of body. Left hand on top. 10-12 are considered one set of techniques. Do 11-12 as one combination

立ち方●右三戦立ち
技●右掌掬い受け、左掌下段底掌落とし
注意点●右掌上（右中心線）、左掌下（左中心線）。ゆっくり。前進と受けと合わせる

Stance ● Right Sanchin Dachi
Tech. ● Right Sukui Uke, Left Gedan Teisho Otoshi
Point ● Right hand on top. Blocks are in center of left/right half of body. Do slowly. Block while stepping forward

第14挙動　　第15挙動

立ち方●右半後屈立ち
技●右掌下段払い、左掌引き手
注意点●三戦立ちから腰を切って半後屈立ち

Stance ● Right Han Kokutsu Dachi

Tech. ● Right Gedan Barai, left Hikite

Point ● Change stance from Sanchin Dachi into Han Kokutsu Dachi using hips

立ち方●右三戦立ち
技●右掌掬い受け、左掌下段底掌落とし
注意点●正中線、右掌上・左掌下。第13〜15挙動は一連の動作。第14〜15挙動は連続で速く

Stance ● Right Sanchin Dachi

Tech. ● Right Sukui Uke, Left Gedan Teisho Otoshi

Point ● Blocks are in center of body. Right hand on top. 13-15 are considered one set of techniques. Do 14-15 as one combination.

二本目　No.2

第 16 挙動	第 17 挙動	第 18 挙動

中間動作

裏側

立ち方●左猫足立ち
技●右掌内受け水月、左平受け
注意点●右足を北西に下げ、猫足と同時に受ける
Stance ● Left Nekoashi Dachi
Tech. ● Put right hand in front of solar plexus after performing Uchi uke. Left Hira Uke
Point ● Pull right foot back toward northwest. Block at the same time as moving into Nekoashi Dachi

立ち方●前足踏み出し
技●右手底掌押し
注意点●左手内小手をこするように押し出す
Stance ● Step forward w/ front foot
Tech. ● Right Teisho Oshi
Point ● Right hand slides up left arm

立ち方●摺り足立ち
技●左上段開甲拳突き、右掌水月
Stance ● Suriashi Dachi
Tech. ● Left Jodan Kaikoken Tsuki. Right palm in fromt of solar plexus

【分解】
Bunkai

二本目（続き）

第 19 挙動　　　第 20 挙動

技●右中段前蹴り
注意点●上肢がブレないように脇を
締める
Tech. ● Right Chudan Maegeri
Point ● Keep arms close to
body. Be careful not to move
upper body

立ち方●右直角四股立ち
技●右開手肘当て、左掌水月
注意点●肘当ては肩より高くならない。気合
Stance ● Right Shiko Dachi 90°
Tech. ● Right Hijiate (open hand). Left hand
is in front of solar plexus
Point ● Hijiate is at shoulder height or lower.
Kiai

第 21 挙動

第 22 挙動

中間動作

裏側

立ち方●左猫足立ち
技●左掌水月水平、右掌引き手
注意点●右足を北西に下げ、半身猫足にしながら開手で構える。第16～21挙動は一連の動作

Stance ● Left Nekoashi Dachi
Tech. ● Lie left palm in front of solar plexus. Right Hlkite
Point ● Pull right foot back toward northwest into Hanmi (hips twisted 45°) Nekoashi Dachi while performing above techniques. 16-21 are considered one set of techniques

立ち方●右猫足立ち
技●左掌内受け水月、右平受け
注意点●左足を北東に下げ、猫足と同時に受ける

Stance ● Right Nekoashi Dachi
Tech. ● Put left hand in front of solar plexus after performing Uchi Uke. Right Hira Uke
Point ● Pull left foot back toward northeast. Block at the same time as moving into Nekoashi Dachi

【分解】
Bunkai

二本目（続き）

三本目　No.3

第 23 挙動　　第 24 挙動　　第 25 挙動

立ち方●前足踏み出し
技●左手底掌押し
注意点●右手内小手をこするように
押し出す
Stance ● Step forward w/ front
foot
Tech. ● Left Teisho Oshi
Point ● Left hand slides up right
arm

立ち方●摺り足立ち
技●右上段開甲拳突き、左掌水月
Stance ● Suriashi Dachi
Tech. ● Right Jodan Kaikoken
Tsuki. Left palm is in front of
solar plexus

技●左中段前蹴り
注意点●上肢がブレないように脇を
しめる
Tech. ● Left Chudan Maegeri
Point ● Keep arms close to
body not to move upper body

第26挙動

第27挙動

中間動作

裏側

立ち方●左直角四股立ち
技●左開手肘当て、右掌水月
注意点●肘当ては肩より高くならない。
気合
Stance ● Left Shiko Dachi 90°
Tech. ● Left Hijiate. Right palm is in front of solar plexus
Point ● Hijiate height is same or lower than shoulder. Kiai

立ち方●右猫足立ち
技●右掌水月水平、左掌引き手
注意点●左足を北東に下げ半身猫足にしながら開手で構える。第22～27挙動は一連の動作
Stance ● Right Nekoashi Dachi
Tech. ● Lie right palm in front of solar plexus. Left Hikite.
Point ● Pull left foot back toward northeast into Hanmi (hips twisted 45°) Nekoashi Dachi. 22-27 are considered one set of techniques

第28拳動　　　第29拳動　　　第30拳動

立ち方●右猫足立ち
技●左廻し受け
注意点●両手底掌引き手、左掌上・右掌下
Stance ● Right Nekoashi Dachi
Tech. ● Mawashiuke left hand on top
Point ● Double Hikite w/ Teisho

立ち方●右猫足立ち
技●両手底掌当て
注意点●左掌上・右掌下
Stance ● Right Nekoashi Dachi
Tech. ● Double arm Teisho Ate
Point ● Left hand on top

立ち方●左三戦立ち
技●左開手中段受け、右手掌引き手
注意点●東に向いて、ゆっくり
Stance ● Left Sanchin Dachi
Tech. ● Left Chudan Uke, right Hikite (open hands)
Point ● Turn toward east, slowly

第31挙動　　　　　第32挙動

中間動作

裏側

立ち方●左三戦立ち
技●右後方肘当て、左拳中段伏せ構え
注意点●腕取り後方肘当て。第30～31挙動は続ける
Stance ● Left Sanchin Dachi
Tech. ● Right Hijiate (rear). Left Chudan Fuse Kamae
Point ● Hijiate to rear after catching opponent's arm. Do 30-31 as one combination

立ち方●右三戦立ち
技●右開手中段受け、左手掌引き手
注意点●右足前進。ゆっくり
Stance ● Right Sanchin Dachi
Tech. ● Right Chudan Uke, left Hikite (open hands)
Point ● Step forward w/ right foot. Do slowly

【分解】
Bunkai

四本目　No.4

第33挙動　第34挙動

立ち方●右三戦立ち
技●左後方肘当て、右拳中段伏せ構え
注意点●腕取り後方肘当て。第32～33挙動は続ける
Stance ● Right Sanchin Dachi
Tech.● Left Hijiate (rear). Right Chudan Fuse Kamae.
Point ● Hijiate to rear after catching opponent's arm. Do 32-33 as one combination

立ち方●四股立ち平角
技●両手掌 肘上腕合わせ
注意点●右掌上・左掌下
Stance ● Shiko Dachi 180°
Tech. ● Put right hand on top of left elbow and left hand under right elbow. Both palms face down
Point ● Right hand on top

第35挙動

第36挙動

第37挙動

中間動作

裏側

立ち方●両膝伸ばし
技●両手掌水平伸ばし
注意点●手掌を下向きに、大の字構え
Stance ● Extend knees
Tech. ● Double arm Suihei Nobashi (extend arms horizontally)
Point ● Palms are facing down. "Dainoji Kamae"

立ち方●両膝伸ばし
技●両手掌直角折り曲げ
注意点●広背筋、下肢を締める
Stance ● Extend knees
Tech. ● Bend arms 90°
Point ● Tense legs and back

立ち方●両膝伸ばし
技●両手掌合わせ
注意点●後頭部で手掌を合わせ真上に伸ばす
Stance ● Extend knees
Tech. ● Put open hands together
Point ● Behind head before extending arms up

【分解】
Bunkai

四本目 （続き）

立ち方●両膝伸ばし
技●両手甲を合わせ、真上に伸ばす
注意点●目線は顎を締め下方
Stance ● Extend knees
Tech. ● Extend arms straight up
Point ● Look down. Tense chin

立ち方●四股立ち平角
技●両手後方肘当て
注意点●腰を落として四股立ち。後
頭部で頭突き。息を吐く
Stance ● Shiko Dachi 180°
Tech. ● Double Hijiate to rear
Point ● Make Shiko Dachi and
head butt to rear. Open mouth
at same time. Exhale

第41挙動	第42挙動	第43挙動

中間動作

裏側

立ち方●四股立ち平角
技●両手後方底掌当て
注意点●目線は下方
Stance ● Shiko Dachi 180°
Tech. ● Double arm Teisho Ate (to rear)
Point ● Look down

立ち方●四股立ち平角
技●後方の相手の両足を抱え込む様に　両手掌下段重ね　右掌上・左掌下
注意点●目線は正面
Stance ● Shiko Dachi 180°
Tech. ● Hands come together at Gedan level (right hand top)
Point ● Look front

立ち方●右前屈立ち
技●両手掌上段交差受け
注意点●両手掌を回転交差
Stance ● Right Zenkutsu Dachi
Tech. ● Double hand Jodan Kosa Uke
Point ● Keep hands crossed while twisting

【分解】
Bunkai

四本目（続き）

五本目　No.5

第44挙動　　　　第45挙動

立ち方●結び立ち
技●両手掌を右回転、左回転、腕取り
注意点●手掌回転は底掌部を支点。真後ろを向いて肘を上
げ、両拳を連鎖
Stance ● Musubidachi
Tech. ● Twist hands right, then left, then grab
opponent's arm
Point ● Wrists are fulcrum of twist and must stay
in contact. Turn 180° while raising elbows and fists

立ち方●両爪先立ち、蹲踞（そんきょ）
技●両拳落とし
注意点●腰を真っ直ぐに落とし両拳を真
下に絞る
Stance ● Sonkyo (stand on balls of
feet)
Tech. ● Double fists Otoshi
Point ● Drop hips straight down
while bringing arm down from the
elbow (don't let elbows open out)

第46挙動	第47挙動	第48挙動

中間動作

立ち方●右前屈立ち
技●右手踵掬い
注意点●前屈は北東方向へやや深め。背中は真っ直ぐ。目線は前方下
Stance ● Right Zenkutsu Dachi
Tech. ● Right Kakato Sukui
Point ● Make deep Zenkutsu Dachi toward northeast. Keep back straight. Look front and down

立ち方●右前屈立ち
技●左底掌膝押さえ
注意点●前屈は北東方向やや深め。背中は真っ直ぐ。腰を締め、目線は前方下
Stance ● Right Zenkutsu Dachi
Tech. ● Left Teisho Hiza Osae
Point ● Make deep Zenkutsu Dachi toward northeast. Keep back straight. Look front and down

立ち方●左前屈立ち
技●左手踵掬い
注意点●前屈は北西方向へやや深め。背中は真っ直ぐ。腰を締め、目線は前方下
Stance ● Left Zenkutsu Dachi
Tech. ● Left Kakato Sukui
Point ● Make deep Zenkutsu Dachi toward northwest. Keep back straight. Look front and down

【分解】
Bunkai

五本目（続き）

第 49 挙動	第 50 挙動	第 51 挙動

立ち方●左前屈立ち
技●右底掌膝押さえ
注意点●前屈は北西方向へやや深め。背中は真っ直ぐ。腰を締め、目線は前方下
Stance ● Left Zenkutsu Dachi
Tech. ● Right Teisho Hiza Osae
Point ● Make deep Zenkutsu Dachi toward northwest. Keep back straight. Look front and down

立ち方●左猫足立ち
技●右廻し受け、両手掌引き手
注意点●右手掌上・左掌下
Stance ● Left Nekoashi Dachi
Tech. ● Mawashiuke Hikite
Point ● Right hand on top

立ち方●左猫足立ち
技●両手底掌当て
注意点●右手掌上・左掌下
Stance ● Left Nekoashi Dachi
Tech. ● Double arm Teisho Ate
Point ● Right hand on top

直って	直って	気を付け

中間動作

裏側

立ち方●結び立ち
注意点●顎を引き、両手は真っすぐ
伸ばして大腿側部に付ける
Stance ● Musubidachi
Point ● Pull chin back. Keep
fingers straight and hands on
outer thight

立ち方●結び立ち
注意点●前方30度位、礼は深すぎ
ない
Stance ● Musubidachi
Point ● Bow forward for 30° .Be
careful not to bow too deeply

立ち方●結び立ち
注意点●顎を引き、両手は真っすぐ
伸ばして大腿側部に付ける
Stance ● Musubidachi
Point ● Pull chin back. Keep
fingers straight and hands on
outer thight

礼 　　　　気を付け

立ち方●結び立ち
注意点●前方 30 度位、礼は深すぎ
ない
Stance ● Musubidachi
Point ● Bow forward for 30°.Be
careful not to bow too deeply

立ち方●結び立ち
注意点●顎を引き、両手は真っすぐ
伸ばして大腿側部に付ける
Stance ● Musubidachi
Point ● Pull chin back. Keep
fingers straight and hands on
outer thight

スーパーリンペイ

一百零八手
Suparinpei

型のポイント

剛柔流の最高位の型に相応しい風格と特徴を秘めた型である。

剛柔流の基本型「三戦」から始まるのは、いかに「三戦」が大切かを示す。

四方向に対して受けの妙味と言われる「廻し受け」で対処し、横の四方、斜めの四方ともにバランスを考慮した対称動作となっているので大変安定した型となっている。

他の型には見られない足底での「回転払い」、「二段蹴り」等高度な技も多い。

演武に際しては、正しい「三戦立ち」、「猫足立ち」の運足、回転、「四股立ち」の転身等、最後にしてなお、基本を重視している。型の緩急のあり方を示した見応えのある型である。

分解動作は全日本空手道剛柔会が制定しているスーパーリンペイ型分解組手（1本～6本）から、一本目、二本目、三本目、四本目、五本目、六本目の一部を掲載している。

As the highest kata in goju-ryu, Suparinpei displays the strongest characteristics and atmosphere of Goju-ryu.

The kata starts with Sanchin, the basic kata of Goju-ryu. This shows how important Sanchin is.

Mawashiuke, often called the most exquisite of blocks, is done in four directions.

This is very balanced kata, because of symmetric movements in four cardinal directions as well as diagonal directions.

It includes advanced techniques not found in other kata such as Kaiten Barai with the sole of the foot and Nidan Keri (double kick).

While performing, great importance is placed on Kihon such as accurate steps in Sanchin Dachi and Nekoashi Dachi, rotation, and changing posision in Shiko Dachi even in this final kata.

Suparinpei shows the ideal pace for the performance of kata, and is really worth seeing.

The Suparinpei Kata Bunkai created by J.K.G.A. contains 6 parts all together. Pictures taken from 1, 2, 3, 4, 5, and 6 are included in the following pages.

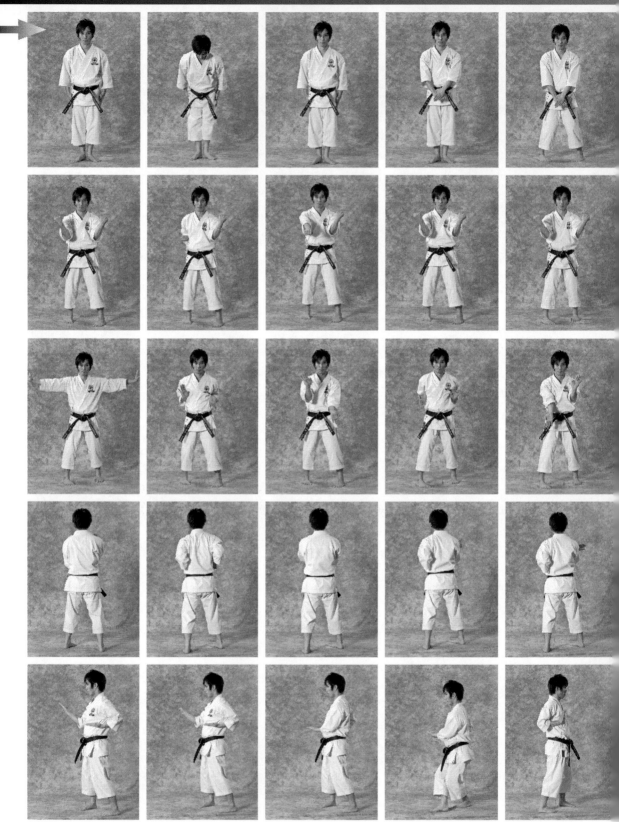

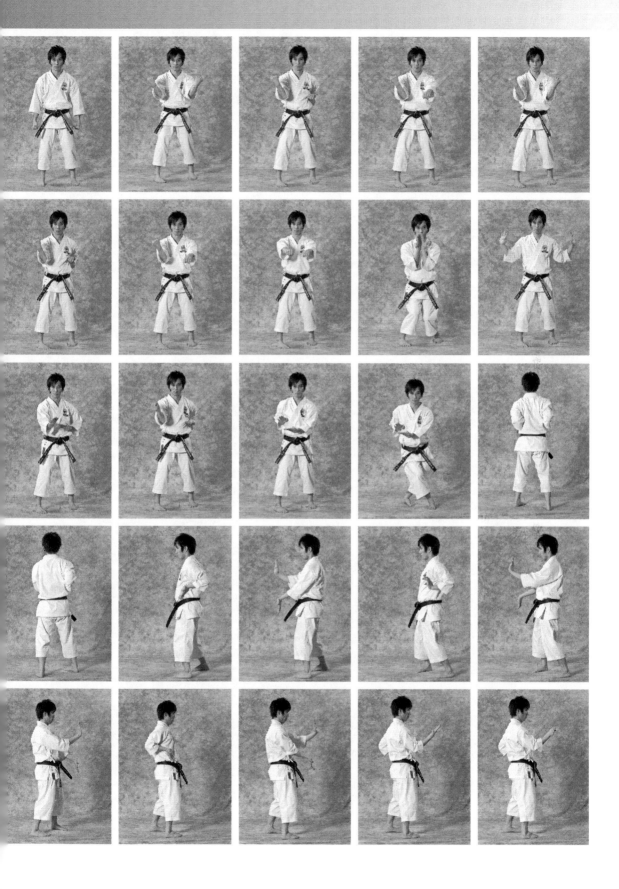

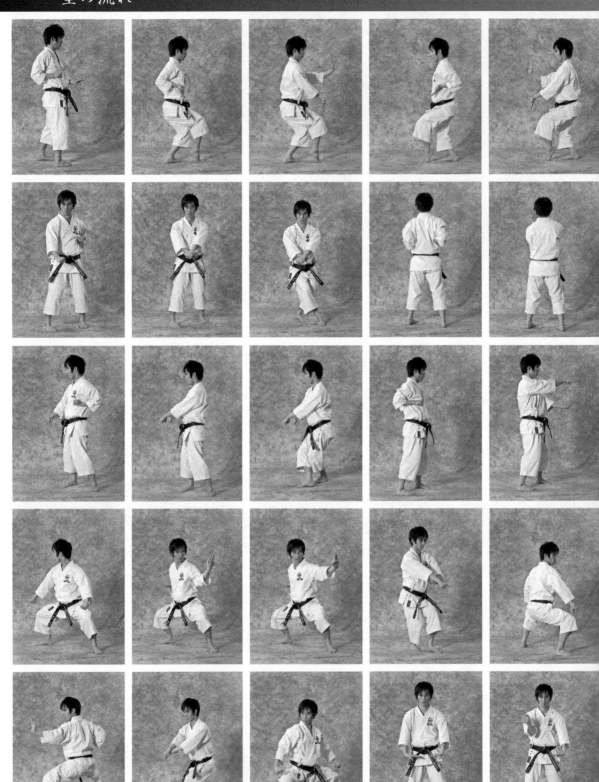

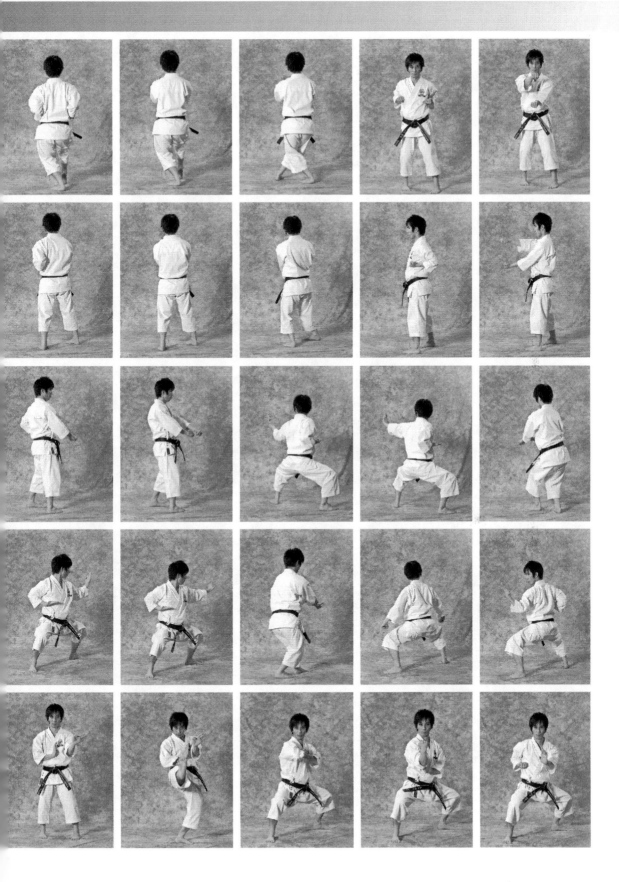

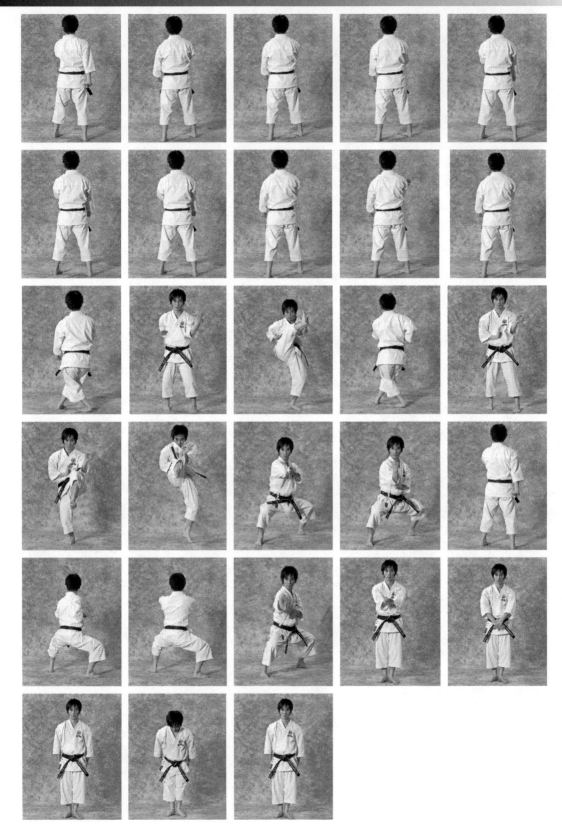

気を付け　　　　　**礼**　　　　　**気を付け**

立ち方●結び立ち
注意点●顎を引き、両手は真っすぐ
伸ばして大腿側部につける
Stance ● Musubidachi
Point ● Pull chin back. Keep
fingers straight and hands on
outer thight

立ち方●結び立ち
注意点●前方 30 度位、礼は深すぎ
ない
Stance ● Musubidachi
Point ● Bow forward for 30° .Be
careful not to bow too deeply

立ち方●結び立ち
Stance ● Musubidachi

用意1 　　　　用意2 　　　　用意3

中間動作

裏側

立ち方●結び立ち
注意点●右掌内側、丹田の前で重ね
集中
息吹●ゆっくり呑
Stance ● Musubidachi
Point ● Right hand on the inside.
Hands are crossed in front of
Tanden
Ibuki ● Inhale slowly

立ち方●平行立ち
注意点●爪先を支点に踵を外に開く
Stance ● Heiko Dachi
Point ● Keep balls of feet in
place and only move heels

立ち方●平行立ち
注意点●両拳は脇を締めながら体側
へ、正拳は真下へ向けて、両肩を落
とす
息吹●ゆっくり吐
Stance ● Heiko Dachi
Point ● Keep elbows against
side of body, fists pointing
straight down, and shoulders
relaxed
Ibuki ● Exhale slowly

第１挙動　第２挙動　第３挙動

立ち方●右三戦立ち
技●三戦の構え。右拳外側より両手
交差
注意点●右足を内側中心線より一歩
前進。三戦の型と同じ
Stance ● Right Sanchin Dachi
Tech. ● Sanchin No Kamae.
Right fist is on outside when
blocking
Point ● Step forward w/ right
foot using an inward curve

立ち方●右三戦立ち
技●左拳　引き手
注意点●三戦の型と同じ
Stance ● Right Sanchin Dachi
Tech. ● Left Hikite
Point ● Same as Sanchin

立ち方●右三戦立ち
技●左拳　正拳突き
注意点●三戦の型と同じ
Stance ● Right Sanchin Dachi
Tech. ● Left Seiken Tsuki
Point ● Same as Sanchin

第4挙動	第5挙動	第6挙動

裏側

立ち方●右三戦立ち
技●左拳　中段横受け
注意点●三戦の型と同じ
Stance ● Right Sanchin Dachi
Tech. ● Left Chudan Yoko Uke
Point ● Same as Sanchin

立ち方●左三戦立ち
技●足だけ前進
注意点●三戦の型と同じ
Stance ● Left Sanchin Dachi
Tech. ● Step forward w/ left foot
Point ● Same as Sanchin

立ち方●左三戦立ち
技●右拳　引き手
注意点●三戦の型と同じ
Stance ● Left Sanchin Dachi
Tech. ● Right Hikite
Point ● Same as Sanchin

第７挙動	第８挙動	第９挙動

立ち方●左三戦立ち 技●右拳　正拳突き 注意点●三戦の型と同じ Stance ● Left Sanchin Dachi Tech. ● Right Seiken Tsuki Point ● Same as Sanchin	立ち方●左三戦立ち 技●右拳　中段横受け 注意点●三戦の型と同じ Stance ● Left Sanchin Dachi Tech. ● Right Chudan Yoko Uke Point ● Same as Sanchin	立ち方●右三戦立ち 技●足だけ前進 注意点●三戦の型と同じ Stance ● Right Sanchin Dachi Tech. ● Step forward w/ right foot Point ● Same as Sanchin

第 10 挙動　　　　第 11 挙動　　　　第 12 挙動

中間動作

裏側

立ち方●右三戦立ち
技●左拳　引き手
注意点●三戦の型と同じ
Stance ● Right Sanchin Dachi
Tech. ● Left Hikite
Point ● Same as Sanchin

立ち方●右三戦立ち
技●左拳　正拳突き
注意点●三戦の型と同じ
Stance ● Right Sanchin Dachi
Tech. ● Left Seiken Tsuki
Point ● Same as Sanchin

立ち方●右三戦立ち
注意点●両手拳を伸ばす
Stance ● Right Sanchin Dachi
Tech. ● Extend arms

第13挙動

立ち方●右三戦立ち
技●両手甲を正中線で合わせ、左右に底掌を張り伸ばす
注意点●両膝を落とすが、両踵は浮かせない
Stance ● Right Sanchin Dachi
Tech. ● Bring backs of hands together in front of center of body. Then extend arms sideways using Teisho
Point ● Bend knees. But not to lift heels off floor

一本目　No.1

第 14 挙動　　　第 15 挙動

中間動作

裏側

立ち方●左三戦立ち
技●右廻し受け
注意点●三戦立ち前進と廻し受けは
同時
Stance ● Left Sanchin Dachi
Tech. ● Mawashiuke right hand
on top
Point ● Step and block at the
same time

立ち方●左三戦立ち
技●両手底掌当て　右掌上・左掌下
注意点●下肢臀部を締めながら
Stance ● Left Sanchin Dachi
Tech. ● Double arm Teisho Ate
right hand on top
Point ● Tense legs and buttocks while striking

【分解】
Bunkai

第 16 挙動　　　　第 17 挙動　　　　第 18 挙動

立ち方●右三戦立ち
技●左廻し受け
注意点●三戦立ち前進と廻し受けは
同時
Stance ● Right Sanchin Dachi
Tech. ● Mawashiuke left hand
on top
Point ● Step and block at the
same time

立ち方●右三戦立ち
技●両手底掌当て　左掌上・右掌下
注意点●下肢臀部を締めながら
Stance ● Right Sanchin Dachi
Tech. ● Double arm Teisho Ate
left hand on top
Point ● Tense legs and buttocks while striking

立ち方●右三戦立ち
技●右掬い受け　左掌引き手
Stance ● Right Sanchin Dachi
Tech. ● Right Sukui Uke, left
Hikite

第19挙動	第20挙動	第21挙動

中間動作

裏側

立ち方●右三戦立ち
技●左掌　斜め貫手　右掌掛け取り
引き手
注意点●左掌は上　右掌は手首を立
てる。貫手の肘は体から離さない
Stance ● Right Sanchin Dachi
Tech. ● Left Nukite (diagonally),
right Kake Tori Hikite
Point ● Left palm facing up.
Bend right wrist up. Keep left
elbow close to body

立ち方●右三戦立ち
技●右掛け取り
Stance ● Right Sanchin Dachi
Tech. ● Right Kake Tori

立ち方●前足交差
注意点●上肢はそのまま
Stance ● Cross front leg in front
Point ● Keep Nukite and Kake
Tori

【分解】
Bunkai

二本目　No.2

第 22 挙動	第 23 挙動	第 24 挙動

立ち方●左三戦立ち
技●右廻し受け
注意点●三戦立ちで回転、北に廻し受け
Stance ● Left Sanchin Dachi
Tech. ● Mawashiuke right hand on top
Point ● Turn toward north in Sanchin Dachi

立ち方●左三戦立ち
技●両手底掌当て　右掌上・左掌下
注意点●下肢臀部を締めながら
Stance ● Left Sanchin Dachi
Tech. ● Double arm Teisho Ate right hand on top
Point ● Tense legs and buttocks while striking

立ち方●右三戦立ち
技●左廻し受け
注意点●三戦立ち前進と廻し受けは同時
Stance ● Right Sanchin Dachi
Tech. ● Mawashiuke left hand on top
Point ● Step and block at the same time

第 25 挙動	第 26 挙動	第 27 挙動

中間動作

裏側

立ち方●右三戦立ち
技●両手底掌当て
注意点●下肢臀部を締めながら
Stance ● Right Sanchin Dachi
Tech. ● Double arm Teisho Ate left hand on top
Point ● Tense legs and buttocks while striking

立ち方●右三戦立ち
技●右掬い受け　左掌引き手
Stance ● Right Sanchin Dachi
Tech. ● Right Sukui Uke, left Hikite

立ち方●右三戦立ち
技●右掛け取り
Stance ● Right Sanchin Dachi
Tech. ● Right Kake Tori

【分解】
Bunkai

第28挙動	第29挙動	第30挙動

立ち方●右三戦立ち
技●左掌　斜め貫手。右掌掛け取り引き手
注意点●左掌は上　右掌は手首を立てる。
貫手の肘は体から離さない
Stance ● Right Sanchin Dachi
Tech. ● Left Nukite (diagonally).
Right Kake Tori Hikite
Point ● Left palm facing up. Bend
right wrist up. Keep left elbow close
to body

立ち方●左三戦立ち
技●右廻し受け
注意点●三戦立ちて西へ転身、廻し受け
Stance ● Left Sanchin Dachi
Tech. ● Mawashiuke right hand on
top
Point ● Turn toward west in Sanchin
Dachi before Mawashiuke

立ち方●左三戦立ち
技●両手底掌当て　右掌上・左掌下
注意点●下肢臀部を締めながら
Stance ● Left Sanchin Dachi
Tech. ● Double arm Teisho Ate
right hand on top
Point ● Tense legs and buttocks
while striking

第31挙動	第32挙動	第33挙動

裏側

立ち方●右三戦立ち	立ち方●右三戦立ち	立ち方●右三戦立ち
技●左廻し受け　両掌引き手	技●両手底掌当て　左掌上・右掌下	技●右掬い受け　左掌引き手
注意点●三戦立ち前進と廻し受けは同時	注意点●下肢臀部を締めながら	Stance ● Right Sanchin Dachi
Stance ● Right Sanchin Dachi	Stance ● Right Sanchin Dachi	Tech. ● Right Sukui Uke, Left
Tech. ● Mawashiuke left hand on top	Tech. ● Double arm Teisho Ate left hand on top	Hikite
Point ● Step and block at the same time	Point ● Tense legs and buttocks while striking	

第 34 拳動   第 35 拳動   第 36 拳動

立ち方●右三戦立ち
技●右掛け取り
Stance ● Right Sanchin Dachi
Tech. ● Right Kake Tori

立ち方●右三戦立ち
技●左掌　斜め貫手。右掌掛け取り引き手
注意点●左掌は上　右掌は手首を立てる。
貫手の肘は体から離さない
Stance ● Right Sanchin Dachi
Tech. ● Left Nukite (diagonally).
Right Kake Tori Hikite
Point ● Left palm facing up. Bend
right wrist up. Keep left elbow close
to body

立ち方●前足交差
注意点●上肢はそのまま
Stance ● Cross feet in front
Tech. ● Keep Nukite and Kake
Tori Hikite

第 37 挙動	第 38 挙動	第 39 挙動

裏側

立ち方●左三戦立ち 技●右廻し受け 注意点●三戦立ちて回転、東に廻し受け Stance ● Left Sanchin Dachi Tech. ● Mawashiuke right hand on top Point ● Turn toward east in Sanchin Dachi	立ち方●左三戦立ち 技●両手底掌当て　右掌上・左掌下 注意点●下肢臀部を締めながら Stance ● Left Sanchin Dachi Tech. ● Double arm Teisho Ate right hand on top Point ● Tense legs and buttocks while striking	立ち方●右三戦立ち 技●左廻し受け 注意点●三戦立ち前進と廻し受けは同時 Stance ● Right Sanchin Dachi Tech. ● Mawashiuke left hand on top Point ● Step and block at the same time

第40挙動	第41挙動	第42挙動

立ち方●右三戦立ち
技●両手底掌当て　左掌上・右掌下
注意点●下肢臀部を締めながら
Stance ● Right Sanchin Dachi
Tech. ● Double arm Teisho Ate left hand on top
Point ● Tense legs and buttocks while striking

立ち方●右三戦立ち
技●右掬い受け　左掌引き手
Stance ● Right Sanchin Dachi
Tech. ● Right Sukui Uke, left Hikite

立ち方●右三戦立ち
技●右掛け取り
Stance ● Right Sanchin Dachi
Tech. ● Right Kake Tori

第43挙動  　　　　第44挙動

中間動作

裏側  　　　　　　　　　　　

立ち方●右三戦立ち
技●左掌　斜め貫手　右掌掛け取り引き手
注意点●左掌は上　右掌は手首を立てる。
貫手の肘は体から離さない
Stance ● Right Sanchin Dachi
Tech. ● Left Nukite, right Kake Tori
Hikite
Point ● Left palm facing up. Bend
right wrist up. Keep left elbow close
to body

立ち方●右猫足立ち
技●左掌廻し受け
注意点●後退しながら廻し受け
Stance ● Right Nekoashi Dachi
Tech. ● Mawashiuke left hand
on top
Point ● Step back while blocking

第 45 挙動　　　　　　　　第 46 挙動

立ち方●右猫足立ち
技●両手底掌当て　左掌上・右掌下
Stance ● Right Nekoashi Dachi
Tech. ● Double arm Teisho Ate
left hand on top

立ち方●左猫足立ち
技●右廻し受け
注意点●前足前進　真後ろ西に回転、廻し受け
Stance ● Left Nekoashi Dachi
Tech. ● Mawashiuke right hand on top
Point ● Step forward w/ front foot, turn toward west before Mawashiuke

三本目　No.3

第 47 挙動　　　　　　　　　　　　第 48 挙動

中間動作

裏側

立ち方●左猫足立ち
技●両手底掌当て　右掌上・左掌下
Stance ● Left Nekoashi Dachi
Tech. ● Double arm Teisho Ate
right hand on top

立ち方●右猫足立ち
技●左廻し受け
注意点●左足を南に寄せて、右足を引きつけながら北に廻し受け
Stance ● Right Nekoashi Dachi
Tech. ● Mawashiuke left hand on top
Point ● Move left foot toward south. Do Mawashiuke toward north while pull right foot in

 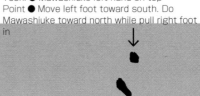

第 49 挙動	第 50 挙動	第 51 挙動

立ち方●右猫足立ち
技●両手底掌当て　左掌上・右掌下
Stance ● Right Nekoashi Dachi
Tech. ● Double arm Teisho Ate
left hand on top

立ち方●前足交差
Stance ● Cross right leg in front

立ち方●左三戦立ち
技●両手拳　引き手。右拳上　左拳下
注意点●北から南に回転。両拳の引き手は、右拳甲は上向き、左拳甲は下向き
Stance ● Left Sanchin Dachi
Tech. ● Double Hikite w/ fists
Point ● Turn toward south. Back of right fist facing up. Back of left fist facing down

第52拳動　第53拳動　第54拳動

中間動作

裏側

立ち方●左三戦立ち
技●両手突き　正中線。右拳上・左拳下
注意点●右拳回旋はしない。左拳は下突き
Stance ● Left Sanchin Dachi
Tech. ● Morote Tsuki right hand on top in center of the body
Point ● Don't twist right fist. Left punch is Shita Tsuki

立ち方●右三戦立ち
技●右止め受け
注意点●右正拳の肘を下段に落とし受け
Stance ● Right Sanchin Dachi
Tech. ● Right Tome Uke
Point ● Drop right elbow down into Gedan Otoshi Uke

立ち方●右三戦立ち
技●左中段正拳突き
注意点●右止め受けはそのまま。上から突く
Stance ● Right Sanchin Dachi
Tech. ● Left Chudan Seiken Tsuki
Point ● Keep right Tome Uke. Punch from above

第55挙動　　　　第56挙動　　　　第57挙動

立ち方●前足交差
Stance ● Cross legs

立ち方●左三戦立ち
技●両手拳　引き手。右拳上・左拳下
注意点●南から北に回転。両拳の引き手
は、右拳甲は上向き、左拳甲は下向き
Stance ● Left Sanchin Dachi
Tech. ● Double Hikite. Right hand
on top
Point ● Turn toward north. Back of
right fist facing up and left facing
down

立ち方●左三戦立ち
技●両手突き　正中線。右拳上・左拳下
注意点●右拳回旋はしない。左拳は下突
き
Stance ● Left Sanchin Dachi
Tech. ● Morote Tsuki right hand on
top in center of body
Point ● Don't twist right fist. Left
punch is Shita Tsuki

第58挙動

第59挙動

第60挙動

中間動作

裏側

立ち方●右三戦立ち
技●右止め受け
注意点●右正拳の肘を下段に落とし受け
Stance ● Right Sanchin Dachi
Tech. ● Right Tome Uke
Point ● Drop right elbow down into Gedan Otoshi Uke

立ち方●右三戦立ち
技●左中段正拳突き
注意点●右止め受けはそのまま。上から突く
Stance ● Right Sanchin Dachi
Tech. ● Left Chudan Seiken Tsuki
Point ● Keep right Tome Uke. Punch from above

立ち方●前足移動
Stance ● Move front foot

第61挙動　　　　第62挙動　　　　第63挙動

立ち方●左三戦立ち
技●両手拳　引き手。右拳上・左拳下
注意点●北から西に転身。両拳の引き手
は、右拳甲は上向き、左拳甲は下向き
Stance ● Left Sanchin Dachi
Tech. ● Double Hikite. Right hand
on top
Point ● Turn toward west. Back of
right fist facing up and left facing
down

立ち方●左三戦立ち
技●両手突き　正中線。右拳上・左拳下
注意点●右拳回旋はしない。左拳は下突
き
Stance ● Left Sanchin Dachi
Tech. ● Morote Tsuki right hand on
top in center of body
Point ● Don't twist right fist. Left
punch is Shita Tsuki

立ち方●右三戦立ち
技●右止め受け
注意点●右正拳の肘を下段に落とし受け
Stance ● Right Sanchin Dachi
Tech. ● Right Tome Uke
Point ● Drop right elbow down into
Gedan Otoshi Uke

第64挙動	第65挙動	第66挙動

中間動作

裏側

立ち方●右三戦立ち
技●左中段正拳突き
注意点●右止め受けはそのまま。上から
突く
Stance ● Right Sanchin Dachi
Tech. ● Left Chudan Seiken Tsuki
Point ● Keep right Tome Uke.
Punch from above

立ち方●前足交差
Stance ● Cross front leg

立ち方●左三戦立ち
技●両手拳　引き手。右拳上・左拳下
注意点●西から東に回転。両手の引き手
は右拳甲は上向き、左拳甲は下向き
Stance ● Left Sanchin Dachi
Tech. ● Double Hikite. Right hand
on top
Point ● Turn toward east. Back of
right fist facing up and left facing
down

第67挙動　第68挙動　第69挙動

立ち方●左三戦立ち
技●両手突き　正中線。右拳上・左拳下
注意点●右拳回旋はしない。左拳は下突き
Stance ● Left Sanchin Dachi
Tech. ● Morote Tsuki right hand on top in center of body
Point ● Don't twist right fist. Left punch is Shita Tsuki

立ち方●右三戦立ち
技●右止め受け
注意点●右正拳の肘を下段に落とし受け
Stance ● Right Sanchin Dachi
Tech. ● Right Tome Uke
Point ● Drop right elbow down into Gedan Otoshi Uke

立ち方●右三戦立ち
技●左中段正拳突き
注意点●右止め受けはそのまま。上から突く
Stance ● Right Sanchin Dachi
Tech. ● Left Chudan Seiken Tsuki
Point ● Keep right Tome Uke. Punch from above

第70挙動	第71挙動	第72挙動

裏側

立ち方●左直角四股立ち
技●左開手中段横受け　右手開手引き手
注意点●東から南東に右足移動
Stance ● Left Shiko Dachi 90°
Tech. ● Left Chudan Yoko Uke and right hikite, w/ open hands
Point ● Step w/ right foot from east to southeast

立ち方●左直角四股立ち
技●左底掌押し
注意点●受けた小手を押し返す
Stance ● Left Shiko Dachi 90°
Tech. ● Left Teiso Oshi
Point ● Push opponent's forearm back after blocking

技●左掌押さえ落とし、右一本拳突き
注意点●右足を直角に踏み込み移動
Tech. ● Left Osae Otoshi, right Ipponken Tsuki
Point ● Step in w/ right foot

【分解】
Bunkai

四本目　No.4

第73挙動	第74挙動	第75挙動

立ち方●右直角四股立ち
技●両手下段鉄槌打ち
注意点●手首のスナップで鉄槌打ち
Stance ● Right Shiko Dachi 90°
Tech. ● Double arm Gedan Tettsui Uchi
Point ● Hit w/ snap

立ち方●左直角四股立ち
技●左開手中段横受け。右手開手引き手
注意点●目線は北西から南東に振り向く
Stance ● Left Shiko Dachi 90°
Tech. ● Left Chudan Yoko Uke and right hikite. w/ open hands
Point ● Look southeast from northwest

立ち方●左直角四股立ち
技●左底掌押し
注意点●受けた小手を押し返す
Stance ● Left Shiko Dachi 90°
Tech. ● Left Teiso Oshi
Point ● Push opponent's forearm back after blocking

四本目（続き）

第76挙動	第77挙動	第78挙動

中間動作

裏側

技●左掌押さえ落とし　右一本拳突き
注意点●右足を直角に踏み込み移動
Tech. ● Left Osae Otoshi, right Ipponken Tsuki
Point ● Step in w/ right foot

立ち方●右直角四股立ち
技●両手下段鉄槌打ち
注意点●手首のスナップで鉄槌打ち
Stance ● Right Shiko Dachi 90°
Tech. ● Double arm Gedan Tettsui Uchi
Point ● Hit w/ snap

立ち方●左直角四股立ち
技●左開手中段横受け　右手開手引き手
注意点●右足を南西に移動
Stance ● Left Shiko Dachi 90°
Tech. ● Left Chudan Yoko Uke and right hikite, w/ open hands
Point ● Step w/ right foot toward southwest

 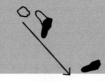 

【分解】
Bunkai

（別角度）

第79挙動	第80挙動	第81挙動

立ち方●左直角四股立ち
技●左底掌押し
注意点●受けた小手を押し返す
Stance ● Left Shiko Dachi 90°
Tech. ● Left Teiso Oshi
Point ● Push opponent's
forearm back after blocking

技●左掌押さえ落とし　右一本拳突き
注意点●右足を直角に踏み込み移動
Tech. ● Left Osae Otoshi, right
Ipponken Tsuki
Point ● Step in w/ right foot

立ち方●右直角四股立ち
技●両手下段鉄槌打ち
注意点●手首のスナップで鉄槌打ち
Stance ● Right Shiko Dachi 90°
Tech. ● Double arm Gedan Tettsui
Uchi
Point ● Hit w/ snap

第82挙動　　　　第83挙動　　　　第84挙動

裏側

立ち方●左直角四股立ち
技●左開手中段横受け　右手開手引き手
注意点●目線は北東から南西に振り向く
Stance ● Left Shiko Dachi 90°
Tech. ● Left Chudan Yoko Uke and right hikite, w/ open hands
Point ● Look southwest from northeast

立ち方●左直角四股立ち
技●左底掌押し
注意点●受けた小手を押し返す
Stance ● Left Shiko Dachi 90°
Tech. ● Left Teiso Oshi
Point ● Push opponent's forearm back after blocking

技●左掌押さえ落とし　右一本拳突き
注意点●右足を直角に踏み込み移動
Tech. ● Left Osae Otoshi, right Ipponken Tsuki
Point ● Step in w/ right foot

第85挙動 第86挙動 第87挙動

立ち方●右直角四股立ち
技●両手下段鉄槌打ち
注意点●手首のスナップで鉄槌打ち
Stance ● Right Shiko Dachi 90°
Tech. ● Double arm Gedan
Tettsui Uchi
Point ● Hit w/ snap

立ち方●左三戦立ち
技●右拳を掌にして、左掌下段払い
Stance ● Left Sanchin Dachi
Tech. ● Left Gedan Barai after
open right hand

立ち方●右三戦立ち
技●右中段掛け受け
Stance ● Right Sanchin Dachi
Tech. ● Right Chudan Kakeuke

四本目（続き）

第88挙動	第89挙動	第90挙動

中間動作

裏側

立ち方●左三戦立ち
技●左中段掛け受け　右掌水月
注意点●第86挙動～第88挙動は
連続動作
Stance ● Left Sanchin Dachi
Tech. ● Left Chudan Kakeuke,
right hand is in front of solar
plexus
Point ● Do 86-88 as one combination

技●右前蹴り
Tech. ● Right Maegeri

立ち方●右四股立ち斜角
技●右横肘当て　左手　肘当て添え
注意点●気合
Stance ● Right Shiko Dachi 45°
Tech. ● Right Yoko Hijiate. Keep
left hand against Hijiate
Point ● Kiai

第91挙動　第92挙動

立ち方●右四股立ち斜角
技●右裏打ち　左掌　肘添え水月
Stance ● Right Shiko Dachi 45°
Tech. ● Right Urauchi. Keep left palm against right elbow in front of solar plexus

立ち方●右四股立ち斜角
技●左掌小手摺り押し　右拳引き手
注意点●ゆっくり小手摺り外し。第89挙動〜92挙動は連続動作
Stance ● Right Shiko Dachi 45°
Tech. ● Left Kote Suri Oshi.
Right Hikite
Point ● When performing Hazushi, slowly rub forearm w/ left hand. Do 89-92 as one combination

四本目（続き）

第93挙動	第94挙動	第95挙動

中間動作

裏側

立ち方●左三戦立ち
技●左中段底掌当て　右後方下段底掌当て
注意点●前足を交差　南から後方北へ回転。速く
Stance ● Left Sanchin Dachi
Tech. ● Left Chudan Teisho Ate, right Gedan Teisho Ate to rear
Point ● Cross front leg and turn 180° from south to north. Hit quickly

立ち方●右三戦立ち
技●両手掌、右掬い受け・左下段払い
注意点●ゆっくり。受けは前進に合わせる
Stance ● Right Sanchin Dachi
Tech. ● Right Sukui Uke, left Gedan Barai (open hands)
Point ● Do slowly. Block while stepping forward

立ち方●右三戦立ち
技●右掌掛け受け、左掌はそのまま
注意点●ゆっくり
Stance ● Right Sanchin Dachi
Tech. ● Right Kakeuke, keep left Gedan Barai
Point ● Slowly

第96挙動	第97挙動	第98挙動

立ち方●右三戦立ち
技●右掌小手絞り
注意点●第94挙動～96挙動はゆっくり連続
Stance ● Right Sanchin Dachi
Tech. ● Kote Shibori w/ open hand
Point ● Do 94-96 slowly as one combination

立ち方●左三戦立ち
技●両手掌、左掬い受け・右下段払い
注意点●ゆっくり。受けは前進に合わせる
Stance ● Left Sanchin Dachi
Tech. ● Left Sukui Uke, right Gedan Barai
Point ● Slowly. Block while stepping forward

立ち方●左三戦立ち
技●左掌掛け受け　右掌はそのまま
立ち方●ゆっくり
Stance ● Right Sanchin Dachi
Tech. ● Left Kakeuke, keep right Gedan Barai
Point ● Slowly

第99挙動	第100挙動	第101挙動

中間動作

裏側

立ち方●左三戦立ち
技●左掌小手絞り
注意点●第97挙動〜99挙動はゆっくり連続
Stance ● Left Sanchin Dachi
Tech. ● Kote Shibori w/ open hand
Point ● Do97-99 slowly as one combination

立ち方●右三戦立ち
技●両手掌、右掬い受け・左下段払い
注意点●ゆっくり。受けは前進に合わせる
Stance ● Right Sanchin Dachi
Tech. ● Right Sukui Uke, left Gedan Barai
Point ● Slowly. Block while stepping forward

立ち方●右三戦立ち
技●右掌掛け受け　左掌はそのまま
立ち方●ゆっくり
Stance ● Right Sanchin Dachi
Tech. ● Right Kakeuke, keep left Gedan Barai
Point ● Slowly

第102挙動	第103挙動	第104挙動

立ち方●右三戦立ち
技●右掌小手絞り
注意点●第100-102挙動はゆっくり連続。第94-96挙動を3回連続
Stance ● Right Sanchin Dachi
Tech. ● Kote Shibori w/ open hand
Point ● Do100-102 slowly as one combination. (Repeat 94-96 three times)

立ち方●前足交差
Stance ● Cross legs

立ち方●左三戦立ち
技●左開手中段横受け、右掌　引き手
Stance ● Left Sanchin Dachi
Tech. ● Left Chudan Yoko Uke, right Hikite (open hands)

五本目　No.5

第105挙動　　第106挙動　　第107挙動

中間動作

裏側

立ち方●左三戦立ち
技●左掛け受け
注意点●第105〜107挙動は連続
動作
Stance ● Left Sanchin Dachi
Tech. ● Left Kakeuke
Point ● Do 105-107 as one
combination

技●右足底中段払い　左掌に当てる
Tech. ● Right Sokutei Chudan
Barai. Hit left palm w/ bottom of
right foot

注意点●足払いの右足を360度回転
Point ● Bring right leg around
360° after Ashibarai

五本目（続き）

第108挙動　　　　第109挙動　　　　第110挙動

技●二段蹴り　その場で飛び上がる
注意点●左前足前蹴り
Tech. ● Nidan Keri (Double kick)
Point ● Left Maegeri

技●二段蹴り
注意点●右足飛び前蹴り
Tech. ● Nidan Keri
Point ● Tobi Maekeri(jumping kick) w/ right foot

立ち方●右四股立ち斜角
技●右横肘当て　左手　肘当て添え
Stance ● Right Shiko Dachi 45°
Tech. ● Right Yoko Hijiate. Keep left hand against Hijiate

五本目　（続き）

第111挙動

第112挙動

中間動作

裏側

立ち方●右四股立ち斜角
技●右裏打ち。左掌　肘添え水月
注意点●第108～111挙動は連続
動作
Stence ● Right Shiko Dachi 45°
Tech. ● Right Urauchi. Keep left
hand against right elbow in front
of solar plexus
Point ● Do 108-111 as one
combination

立ち方●左三戦立ち
技●左中段底掌当て　右後方下段底掌当
て
注意点●前足を交差、南から後方北へ回
転。速く
Stance ● Left Sanchin Dachi
Tech. ● Left Chudan Teisho Ate.
Right Gedan Teiso Ate to rear
Point ● Cross legs and turn 180°.
Do quickly

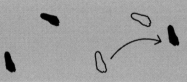

六本目

第 113 挙動　　　　第 114 挙動

立ち方●左四股立ち斜角
技●両手掛け受け。右掌　開手引き手、甲が上
注意点●右後足踵を内旋させ、左足を斜角に前
進。掛け受けは右掌内掛け、左掌外掛け
Stance ● Left Shiko Dachi 45°
Tech. ● Double arm Kake Uke.Right Hikite's
palm facing down
Point ● Bring right heel in, then step
forward 45° into Shiko Dachi. First, block
right Uchi Kakeuke, then left Soto Kakeuke

立ち方●左四股立ち斜角
技●右手横貫手　左手開手上腕添え
注意点●気合
Stance ● Left Shiko Dachi 45°
Tech. ● Right Yoko Nukite. Keep
left palm on top of right upper arm
Point ● Kiai

六本目（続き）

第115挙動 　　 直って 　　 直って

中間動作

裏側

立ち方●右四股立ち斜角
技●鶴頭受け「犬の構え」
注意点●左足を右に交差、180度回
転。右鶴頭・左鶴頭を内旋、当て
Stance ● Right Shiko Dachi 45°
Tech. ● Kakuto Uke. Inu no
Kamae
Point ● Cross left leg in front
of right. Turn 180° .Rotate both
Kakuto inside into Ate

立ち方●結び立ち
注意点●顎を引き、両手は真っすぐ
伸ばして大腿側部に付ける
Stance ● Musubidachi
Point ● Pull chin back. Keep
fingers straight and hands on
outer thight

立ち方●結び立ち
注意点●前方30度位、礼は深すぎ
ない
Stance ● Musubidachi
Point ● Bow forward for 30° .Be
careful not to bow too deeply

気を付け　　　礼　　　気を付け

立ち方●結び立ち
注意点●顎を引き、両手は真っすぐ
伸ばして大腿側部に付ける
Stance ● Musubidachi
Point ● Pull chin back. Keep
fingers straight and hands on
outer thight

立ち方●結び立ち
注意点●前方 30 度位、礼は深すぎ
ない
Stance ● Musubidachi
Point ● Bow forward for 30° .Be
careful not to bow too deeply

立ち方●結び立ち
注意点●顎を引き、両手は真っすぐ
伸ばして大腿側部に付ける
Stance ● Musubidachi
Point ● Pull chin back. Keep
fingers straight and hands on
outer thight

おわりに

　剛柔流の型修錬は「三戦」から始まり、「転掌」に終わると言われております。

　初心者は太極（タイキョク）、ゲキサイの基本動作より始まり、同時に「三戦」も指導を受けます。しかし、競技大会を目標にした練習を主体としているクラブ等では、「三戦」・「転掌」を競技会で選択する事は無いので、これらの練習が大変疎かになっていると思われます。

　流祖宮城長順先生は戦地に赴く弟子達に、「三戦」・「転掌」だけは毎日必ず修錬する様申されたそうです。宮城長順先生より教えを受けた会祖山口剛玄先生も滝行等の荒業を通して「三戦」・「転掌」にこそ剛柔流の極意があり、心身苦境の折に行えば、気力と活力を見出し、生命力がみなぎると云っておられます。

　「三戦」・「転掌」の修錬はすなわち剛柔流空手道修業者の血肉となり、エネルギーとなる元を習得する型であって、養命法としての修身型と言っても過言ではありません。

　「三戦」・「転掌」共に剛柔流独特の立ち方、「三戦立ち」によって下肢の締めと緩みを行い、呼吸法を伴って筋の締め、丹田集中を計り、呼吸の呑吐と力の抜き差しを以って剛柔の境地を体感し、立禅として精神の集中を計ります。

　"剛柔流空手道修錬者は入門より３ヵ年間は「三戦」の型のみ"と言い伝えられておりますが、それ程、重要な型なのです。

　西洋医学によって生物による酸素、二酸化炭素のガス交換が証明され、呼吸の重要性が認識されただけではなく、スポーツ医学においても有酸素、無酸素運動が研究され全てのスポーツに有効な知識として活用されておりますが、中国拳法をルーツとする剛柔流空手道は古来より呼吸と体を重視し、古典武術誌である武備志「拳八句」の文中"法剛柔呑吐"（この世の全ては剛（陽）と柔（陰）から成り立つ）から流名として引用された「剛」と「柔」は「呑吐」で表す呼吸をも含めて全て天然の理に適っております。

　「三戦」・「転掌」で習得した剛柔流資質をもって他の開手型に臨み、点から線、線から円、円から球への境地を求めて下さい。

Closing

Training in Goju-ryu kata is said to start with Sanchin and finish with Tensho.

Beginners begin to study the basic movements of Taikyoku and Gekisai at the same time as Sanchin is taught to them.

However, at some clubs where training focuses on practice for competition, the practice of Sanchin and Tensho tends to be neglected because they are not used for kata competition.

It is said that Chojun Miyagi sensei, the founder of Goju-ryu, had told his students before their departure for the battlefield to make sure to train at least Sanchin and Tensho everyday.

The founder and grand master Gogen Yamaguchi sensei, who studied under Chojun Miyagi sensei, through various austerities like standing under a waterfall, came to the conclusion that the essence of Goju-ryu exists in Sanchin and Tensho.

Even when things become physically or mentally challenging, one can find will power, energy, and be full of life force through the practice of Sanchin and Tensho.

The practice of Sanchin and Tensho indeed nourishes Goju-ryu Karatedo students' bodies and souls. It is no exaggeration to say that these kata are used for building one's energy and maintaining one's health.

In both Sanchin and Tensho, we tense and relax the lower limbs in Sanchin Dachi, tense muscles and concentrate on Tanden with breathing, and finally, aim at attaining the Goju state of mind by Don-To (inhale and exhale) and controlling the balance of tension and relaxation.

Training in this manner is a form of Zen, aimed at mental concentration.

These are such important kata that it is said "Goju-ryu students must study only Sanchin kata for three months after beginning training".

Western medical science has proven the exchange of oxygen and carbon dioxide by living things.

Also, sports science has investigated aerobic / anaerobic exercise and applied this knowledge to be more effective in training for all kinds of sports.

Goju-ryu Karatedo, originated in Chinese martial arts, has emphasized the importance of breathing methods from ancient times.

The name of Goju-ryu was taken from " 法剛柔呑吐 ("Ho Go Ju Don To", all things of this world are made from Go, the positive and Ju, the negative) " written in "Ken Hakku" in Chinese historical records about martial arts, titled "Bubishi".

Go and Ju (in breathing expressed as Don-To) are all in accordance to the laws of nature.

I wish for you to try the other Kaishu Kata with a higher level gained through the practice of Sanchin and Tensho so as to move from "the point " to "the line", "the line" to "the circle", and finally, "the circle" to "the sphere".

監修・演武　Supervisor, Demonstrator

山口 剛史 （本名　紘史）
Goshi Hirofumi Yamaguchi

1942 年 9 月 28 日、満洲　新京にて誕生

全日本空手道剛柔会会祖・山口剛玄の三男として、父を補佐し、国内外の指導に
あたる。

1990 年、「全日本空手道剛柔会」、「国際空手道剛柔会」宗家として会長・最高
師範に就任。

（財）全日本空手道連盟公認　全国指導員、全国審判員、資格審査委員

世界空手道連合　元国際審判員

（財）日本体育協会　上級コーチ、A 級スポーツ指導員

Born on September 28, 1942 in Manchukuo.

He is the third son of Gogen Yamaguchi, the founder and grand master of the
Japan Karatedo Gojukai Association. He has taught both domestically and
overseas helping his father.

In 1990, he became the president and head instructor of the Japan Karatedo
Gojukai Association (J.K.G.A.) and the International Karatedo Gojukai
Association (I.K.G.A.)

Japan Karatedo Federation Instructor, Referee, and Examiner

W.U.K.O. Internatinal referee (retired)

JASA coach, JASA instructor

演武 Demonstrator

斉藤 彰宏
Akihiro Saito

1969 年 2 月 23 日生
6 歳より空手道を修業、高校生・大学生時代は
各種選手権大会、国体等で優勝、入賞。
全日本空手道連盟ナショナルチーム在籍中、各
種国際大会、国際交流遠征に参加。
全日本空手道剛柔会理事、強化委員
師範錬士五段。

Born on February 23, 1969. Started karate at
age 6. During his years as a high school and
university student, he won 1st place at many
championships including national events.
Was a member of the J.K.F. national team and
participated in international competitions
Director of J.K.G.A., member of coaching
comitee
5 dan, Shihan Renshi

演武 Demonstrator

山口 剛平 (本名 たかひら)
Gohei Takahira Yamaguchi

1976 年 2 月 14 日生
幼少 4 歳より祖父山口剛玄、父山口剛史の指
導を受け、国際空手道剛柔会世界大会・分解組
手優勝、型第 3 位。全日本空手道剛柔会全国大
会型 4 回連続優勝。
国際空手道剛柔会・全日本空手道剛柔会指導者
として国内外指導。
全日本空手道剛柔会事務局次長、四段助教。

Born on February 14, 1976. Studied karate
under his grandfather Gogen Yamaguchi and
his father Goshi Yamaguchi from the age of 4.
Won 1st place in Bunkai Kumite, and 3rd place
in Kata at the I.K.G.A. World Championships.
Won 1st place 4 years in a row at the J.K.G.A.
All Japan Championships, in individual kata.
Vice bureau chief of J.K.G.A.
4 dan, Jokyo

Author

Goshi Yamaguchi

Japan Karatedo Gojukai Association

1-16-23 Zempukuji Suginamiku, Tokyo 167-0041 Japan

http://www.karatedo.co.jp/goju-ryu

Publisher

CHAMP Co., Ltd.

4-19-3-2F Koenjiminami Suginamiku, Tokyo 166-0003 Japan

http://www.champ-shop.com

全日本空手道剛柔会　剛柔流型教本（下巻）

2009 年 11 月 30 日　第 1 刷発行

著　者　　全日本空手道剛柔会　山口剛史

発行者　　井出将周

発行所　　株式会社チャンプ

〒 166-0003　東京都杉並区高円寺南 4-19-3

総和第二ビル 2 階

販売部　03（3315）3190

編集部　03（3315）5051

印刷　新晃社

Made in United States
Troutdale, OR
12/09/2023

15596284R00113